# Conversations About Language & Culture

# Conversations About

# LANGUAGE & CULTURE

Edited by Howard Burton

**R Ideas Roadshow**
INTELLIGENT. INQUISITIVE. INTERNATIONAL.

Ideas Roadshow conversations present a wealth of candid insights from some of the world's leading experts, generated through a focused yet informal setting. They are explicitly designed to give non-specialists a uniquely accessible window into frontline research and scholarship that wouldn't otherwise be encountered through standard lectures and textbooks.

Over 100 Ideas Roadshow conversations have been held since our debut in 2012, covering a wide array of topics across the arts and sciences.

All Ideas Roadshow conversations are available both as part of a collection or as an individual eBook.

See www.ideasroadshow.com for a full listing of all titles.

# Contents

**SIGN LANGUAGE LINGUISTICS**
**A CONVERSATION WITH CAROL PADDEN**

**PERSPECTIVES ON MASS COMMUNICATION**
**A CONVERSATION WITH DENIS MCQUAIL**

**THE VALUE OF VOICE**
**A CONVERSATION WITH NICK COULDRY**

# Textual Note

The contents of this book are based upon separate filmed conversations with Howard Burton and each of the five featured experts.

**Michael Berry** is Professor of Contemporary Chinese Cultural Studies and Director of the UCLA Center for Chinese Studies. This conversation occurred on September 19, 2014.

**David Bellos** is the Director of the Program in Translation and Intercultural Communication at Princeton University, where he is also Professor of French and Comparative Literature. This conversation occurred on June 14, 2012.

**Carol Padden** holds the Sanford I. Berman Chair in Language and Human Communication at UC San Diego. This conversation occurred on September 25, 2014.

**Denis McQuail** (1935-2017) was Emeritus Professor at the University of Amsterdam and Visiting Professor at the University of Southampton. He is one of the most influential scholars in the history of mass communication studies. This conversation occurred on April 28, 2014.

**Nick Couldry** is Professor of Media, Communications and Social Theory in the Department of Media and Communications at LSE. This conversation occurred on April 29, 2014.

**Howard Burton** is the creator and host of Ideas Roadshow and was Founding Executive Director of Perimeter Institute for Theoretical Physics.

# Preface

Language, it is often said, is the thing that makes us human—the one feature that truly sets us apart from our fellow non-human travellers on the planet. But it is not so much language per se, of course, that distinguishes us, but rather what we *do* with it.

Because it is one thing to examine the human brain and try to deduce how it is so particularly hard-wired for language—which, as it happens, occurs quite frequently within Ideas Roadshow conversations with cognitive scientists such as Ellen Bialystok, Victor Ferreira, Greg Hickok, Martin Monti and others—and quite another to look at how our biological predilection for words and phrases manifests itself in the cultural realm, which is the subject of this collection.

We begin with two scholars: **Michael Berry**, Director of the UCLA Center for Chinese Studies and **David Bellos**, Professor of French and Director of Princeton University's Program in Translation and Intercultural Communication. Both are highly regarded literary translators whose manifold experiences respectively translating French and Chinese masterworks into English have naturally influenced their appreciation of the subtleties of language that would otherwise be taken for granted.

Michael gives us a revealing, first-hand glimpse of what a translator's "day job" is really like:

> *"When I'm translating dialogue, for example, I'll often speak aloud just to double-check whether people actually talk like that in English, and try to figure out what the perfect equivalent is for capturing the nuance of the original. I think that you have to have a sensitivity of both languages to really capture how someone would express that*

*idea, or thought, or emotion, in the other language. I think that's key to being successful as a translator.*

*"A lot of people talk about 'faithful' translations or 'literal' translations. Often, to create the most faithful translation you have to betray the literal meaning in order to get at that faithful spirit. In Chinese, for example, a very common greeting that people will say to each other is literally, 'Have you eaten?' But you wouldn't say that in a Western country. If I saw you on the street, I wouldn't say, 'Howard, have you eaten?' It would sound very weird. A far better translation would be something like, 'How's it going?' because you want to capture that spirit. They weren't actually asking if you had eaten. It's just a greeting.*

*"You always have to constantly navigate between being faithful to the original and making it readable. That's the tightrope that you're always walking as a translator: between faithfulness to the original and readability to your target audience. Some translators are more on one side than the other. There's no one answer to this."*

David, meanwhile, intriguingly describes how the very act of translating French literature has led him to re-evaluate and re-assess his understanding of his native language.

*"It's a dialogic experience, it goes two ways. I'm sure that my command of the English language and my ability to write has been formed by all these foreign writers that I've had to translate. They've made me learn different things and different nooks and crannies of English.*

*"Years ago, when I started translating Georges Perec, it was just obvious to me to translate into English. I know what English is. English is what I write. But 25 years later, I don't know what English is anymore. I'm much less sure of my ground in saying, 'This is English and this isn't' or 'This is good English or this isn't', or even, indeed, 'This is British and this is American,' because there are all sorts of strange crossovers."*

None of these insights would be particularly shocking to **Carol Padden**, an internationally renowned linguist at UC San Diego.

Following in the footsteps of the hugely innovative sign-language linguist Bill Stokoe, Carol has spent years carefully examining the correspondence between the inherently multi-modal nature of language and the associated information being conveyed.

In particular, she describes how gesture—once avoided by sign language linguists who were understandably concerned that it might distract from the independent recognition of sign language as a bona fide language—is now recognized by all as an essential signpost to unravel the subtleties between different types of linguistic information.

*"The modality is different between speech and sign language, but both are about conveying categorical information. Gesture is about conveying something that's more continuous, more analogic. But language is purposefully not analogic. It's more categorical.*

*"Sometimes, if you want to show a particular kind of distance, signers will use gesture to show if something is bigger than or smaller than something else. These are the signs for 'big' and 'small', but with 'small' I'm not really showing you how small, and the same applies to 'big'. If I wanted to show you how small something is, I might make a gesture that uses space accordingly, the same as if I wanted to show you how big something is.*

*"Again, that's why we think of language use as multi-modal. Languages have rich resources, but you end up using just a subset of that. Like I said, some languages have clicks, some have whistles, some use a lot more gesture—like in the Mediterranean area, for example, as well as in Arabic countries. In southern Europe they use a lot more gesture than in northern Europe.*

*"Much of that is shaped by culture and community. Many of these things people once thought were universal, but now we're beginning to really understand how to describe diversity."*

Lastly, we turn to another topic entirely: the particular way that language is used and abused by the powers that be in society, from the social to the cultural to the political, bringing us inevitably to the role of the media—old media, new media, social media—in our everyday lives.

This is a subject that both **Denis McQuail** and **Nick Couldry** have spent the vast majority of their careers pondering in great detail.

McQuail, a pioneering scholar in the history of mass communication studies who sadly passed away several years after our conversation, describes how we need to pay careful attention to the notion of "mass media" in order to penetrate how communication actually works, a fundamental insight that those who are determined to assure us of the "revolutionary power" of their new communication technology are often keen to misrepresent.

> *"It became fairly clear that much communication was mediated through personal contacts. Even mass media themselves, although they seemed to be directly received by many people at the same time, are, in fact, received in contexts of family circles or friend circles. They are discussed. They enter into conversation. They are filtered through all kinds of barriers in the social circles of particular groups in society.*

> *"Even today, it remains the case that we have to look at how communication is taking place without reference to the technologies; and that applies to new media and social media, as much as anything else. They are generally looked at in isolation from the social relations that really underlie the use of such technologies. Partly that's because that's what the industry wants. That is what the development of the technology requires: that they can make claims for social consequences without reference to any fundamental concern, or knowledge of precisely where they fit into people's lives."*

This near-ritualistic overhyping of the "transformative" impact of new communications technology is also a subject near and dear to Nick Couldry's heart, but for him the twinning of technophilia with a willingness to abandon our interpretive faculties has singularly pernicious implications for our modern world, citing what he calls "the myth of big data" as a particular case in point:

*"This is a myth that's coming at us quite quickly. It is, in a sense, in a sequence with the older myths about our lives needing to be organized around central media, which I have been talking about. But, in a way, it's of a different sort because it's taking over the whole of the scientific establishment as well. It's not that big data as such is a myth. Clearly there are now capacities to do massive parallel calculations of millions of simultaneous equations generating results, which could not be predicted, but which appear to be able to predict other forms of things we want to understand.*

*"The scale of the interpretative task is now unimaginably large. That poses a challenge for the sociological imagination. I stress the word "imagination" because there is a risk—this is common idea in a lot of airport books about the wonders of big data—that the academy itself will get taken over by a view that the challenge now for the sciences and the social sciences is just to do more and more calculations, faster and faster, more and more parallel, to generate proxies which will create—although we won't understand what they mean—means of predicting this or that thing that we do want to understand, or we do want to follow, and we'll just plug the data in and rely on that. We'll give up on the act of interpretation.*

*"As a model of understanding society, and therefore as a model of governments looking over the shoulders of social scientists and understanding what they're trying to govern, this is truly catastrophic, because it erases the space of the human subject and the subject that's trying to interpret that other human subject. It discounts what we know about what matters in our lives together. This is a deeply disabling view of social science and it directly contradicts the view of Weber for whom sociology was the science of interpreting human action."*

The links between language and culture are multi-faceted, often counter-intuitive, and invariably maddeningly complex. But they should never be ignored.

# China, Culturally Speaking

A conversation with Michael Berry

# Introduction

*Living Values*

How does a jazz-obsessed teenager in suburban New Jersey wind up as an internationally-renowned Chinese literary translator and film scholar?

That was the first question I wanted answered when I sat down to chat with Michael Berry. There were plenty of other topics to investigate, of course—the current state of Chinese literature and film, the personal experiences of translating, censorship in China, the evolving relationship of China and Hollywood, to name but a few—and I was determined to get to as many of those as possible. But first things first: how did a guy like Michael become an authority on contemporary Chinese culture in the first place?

*"A key for me was my high-school English teacher, Mr Jensen, who had such a profound influence on my life. He was a large, burly guy who often wore flannel shirts and had a big scruffy beard—he looked almost like a lumberjack—and in class he would do things that were a little bit different from any other teacher.*

*"The real game-changer for me happened one day when he asked all of us to write down our values on a piece of paper. He said, 'Just write down whatever is most important to you, whether it's your relationship with your grandmother, or your health—whatever it is, just write down what's important to you.' Then he told us to keep that with us in our notebooks and bring it to class every day; and that was it.*

*"A couple of weeks later, he started a second assignment for us, which was to keep a daily journal. In the morning, we were to write down what we had planned for that day. Then, before we went to bed, we*

*had to take note of what we did and didn't accomplish, assessing what our progress was for the day.*

*"For several weeks, maybe even a few months, we did that every day. Then one day he asked us to bring the journal to school and bring out that piece of paper with our values on it and compare the two. That was the end of the exercise. He didn't give us any lesson that accompanied the exercise: he just left it with us to draw our own conclusions.*

*"For me, that was a profound moment, because I compared the two and there was a huge discrepancy. It was very clear that there were only two options. One was to look in the mirror and face the fact that most people out there, myself included, are lying to themselves. When it comes to those values we say are so important to us, we aren't, in reality, living them or incorporating them into our lives. So you have to admit that you're lying to yourself. That's the first option.*

*"The more difficult option is to change your life, to change your daily actions in a fundamental and radical way that pulls them into the orbit of your values.*

*"I was probably 17 when I had this experience, and for me that was just a game-changer. It wasn't immediate, but I think that really started to change the gears of my mind, in a way."*

From that point forwards, he began reading voraciously, exposing himself as fast as he could to as many great works of literature as he could get his hands on, correspondingly changing his college major from music to philosophy. But books were only the beginning.

*"I started thinking about how these books had such an incredible impact on me; and I was also aware of the fact that at the age of 18 I could only speak English, I had only lived in the United States, I had only seen one side of things. I went to the study-abroad office to start looking into opportunities to go abroad. They ended up making an exception for me and let me go to China for my sophomore year when I was 19. Usually they want you to wait until your junior year, but I kept going there and pleading my case, and they eventually let me go."*

One year in Nanjing was followed by another in Taiwan. Soon Michael had switched majors again—this time to Chinese Studies—and he had thrown himself into this new and captivating world with all of the passion and dedication he could muster. Mere months after having been a jazz-fusion aficionado devouring the Western literary canon, he found himself keenly delving into Chinese pop music and working through the short stories of Lu Xun.

Before starting a PhD at Columbia in Chinese literature, he decided to try his hand at translating a novel, hardly the sort of thing that your average beginning graduate student would even consider. But Michael, customarily, simply dove in.

*"There was a novel I had read in Taiwan called To Live by Yu Hua, which had also been made into a film by Zhang Yimou, probably China's best known director. I wrote a fax to Yu Hua and he gave me the rights, so I translated it that summer. It was done in a couple of months."*

In fact, Michael told me, that continues to be his pattern with all of his literary translation work: rather than being commissioned to do a work, he simply contacts the authors directly.

When I asked him how he decides on a particular work to translate, he had this to say:

*"At the heart of it is this almost primal urge: I need to translate this book. I just feel such a connection with the work, and am over-whelmed with its power and impact—it's definitely a very emotional experience. Then there's the sense that, in one way or another, it was a contemporary classic, or perhaps had the potential to be a classic. It was a work that had already received a certain degree of attention and enjoyed wide readership in the Chinese market, a work that had resonated with Chinese readers in a way that I believed could cross boundaries and also resonate with international readers. In short, it would be meaningful, in a way that goes back to what I was talking about earlier. It seemed more meaningful to do these translations than not to do them.*

*"This goes back to Mr Jensen and making that choice to change your life and live in accordance with your values. A lot of my translations were driven by an attempt to manifest some of those values, trying to leave something behind that could hopefully make an impact on someone."*

At some level, then, Michael's achievements don't really have anything to do with either China or New Jersey. They speak directly to all of us.

# The Conversation

# I. From New Jersey to Nanjing

*Discovering another world*

**HB**: The obvious question is, how did you become somebody who is so deeply immersed in Chinese culture—not just Chinese film, but Chinese literature too? You're a highly regarded translator, you teach Chinese cultural studies at a premier university. How did that all start for you?

**MB**: It was a somewhat convoluted journey. When I was in college, I spent five years doing my undergraduate degree at four different universities—a year to a year and a half at each one—and I switched majors three times.

I started in a small state college in New Jersey called William Paterson College—now William Paterson University—where I was a Jazz Studies major. When I was in high school I had long hair and I wanted to be a jazz musician. That was my thing.

It was not too long after starting college, when I was still at William Paterson, that I switched to philosophy. But during the first semester of my freshman year at college, I went to the study abroad office at William Paterson and said, "*Sign me up.*" I really wanted to get out there and see the world.

**HB**: Just anywhere? Did you have any particular preference at that point?

**MB**: Well, I knew I wanted to go somewhere, so I figured, *How could I really go wrong?* But I also wanted to do something completely different from the Greco-Roman cultural roots that were so influential in

American and most European cultures. I really wanted to try to avoid that route and open my mind in a new way.

I remember asking about programs in the Middle East, Egypt, India, Japan, and China. Those were the countries that I was really interested in going to.

I have a brother who's four years older than me. When I was in high school, he was in college and studied in Japan for about two and a half years. I saw how that experience transformed his life. I wasn't set on going to Japan as well, but I definitely wanted to take advantage of that study-abroad experience. I saw what that did for him, and it just seemed stupid to not take advantage of this really fundamental aspect of a college education.

Even now, when I deal with students here, I'm always encouraging them to take advantage of study-abroad programs, get out there and open up their minds in entirely new ways and learn a new language.

A language isn't just a kind of hardware, it's a key that's going to open up a door to a whole other perspective on the world. It's a way of looking at different cultures. When you write in another language, you write and think in a different way. It's really just a different perspective. If you look at news broadcasts in other languages, the way that news is reported is very different.

**HB**: I'd like to back up a little bit and trace your history a little more clearly. You started off as a jazz major, but in the back of your mind you were thinking that you'd like to open your mind up to new perspectives and travel. You signed up for a study-abroad program. Somewhere along the way you gave up on jazz, at least as a major, and switched to philosophy.

Were you still playing jazz, even though you had switched majors? Was jazz still a part of the way you defined yourself? And secondly, what did you find exciting or interesting about philosophy? What was going through your mind when you were doing all of this?

**MB**: Let me backtrack a little bit. I played bass in high school, and for several years that's all I did. I would practice six or seven hours a day.

I studied with this incredible teacher, Dave LaRue, who had played with Joe Satriani, Steve Morse, and a bunch of jazz-fusion bands. So I'd pay kids who were older than me and had their driver's licenses to drive me to go and take lessons with this incredible musician.

**HB**: Where was this?

**MB**: Suburban New Jersey: Freehold. The interesting thing is that same drive that I put into studying a musical instrument, that almost obsessive devotion to doing something and doing it well, is something that never changed. I just took that focus and moved it to different places throughout my life. At that stage, it happened to be music: that's what I was enraptured by, and that's what I wanted.

Before that it was art. I used to draw and paint and I won all these awards when I was a little kid for drawings. That was in my elementary school days—I had a private art tutor and I was entering county fairs and things, but it was that same devotion that I've carried with me my whole life. I just put it into art first and later applied it to music.

I know it might seem like big leaps going from jazz to philosophy and then Chinese. A key for me throughout was my high school English teacher, Mr (Dennis) Jensen, who had such a profound influence on my life. He was a large, burly guy who often wore flannel shirts and had a big scruffy beard—he looked almost like a lumberjack—and in class he would do things that were a little bit different from any other teacher. Every once in a while he would pose questions that were just a little bit outside the box.

For example, one day during my college prep English course he asked, "*How many of you are planning on going to college?*" and every kid in the class raised their hand. Then he asked, "*Why?*" and nobody could answer that question.

Of course he wasn't trying to discourage anyone from going to college or anything like that. He was just trying to make us really think about it. You shouldn't be doing things just because society tells you that in a middle-class, suburban, New Jersey neighbourhood, you go to high school, then you go to college, then you get married and have kids. You shouldn't just accept certain societal norms because everybody else is doing it, or because your parents say so. You should ask yourself what your true calling is.

Mr Jensen would tell us stories about how he and his wife were together for years before they formally got married. I remember one classmate asking, "*Why would you do that?*" It was so strange for this one girl in the class to hear him say that. And he just replied, "*Well, with the love and commitment that my wife and I had for each other, we felt that, in and of itself, was the core of our relationship; and to have a religious, legal, or state entity somehow authenticate or make that official was not only unnecessary, but it was almost a defilement of our relationship.*" Of course, half the class thought this was heresy—you could see it in their faces—but for me, those little moments were like someone kind of shaking me awake.

**HB**: A glimpse outside of normal constraints.

**MB**: Exactly. He would do things like that throughout class. He introduced us to books unlike anything I'd ever read before, like Kurt Vonnegut's *Slaughterhouse Five* or Hermann Hesse's *Demian*. He showed us Joseph Campbell's *The Power of Myth*. All of these videos or books were slowly opening something up within me.

I developed a personal relationship with him because one of our neighbours was a schoolteacher and would give me a ride to school, so I'd show up an hour early because that teacher would go in to prep. I started off just sitting on the floor next to my locker reading, but one day Mr Jensen invited me into his room and we would just talk. We talked about music mostly, and through these informal chats every morning he became, not quite a father figure, but perhaps something like that. He had that kind of place in my life during that period.

The real game-changer for me happened one day when he asked all of us to write down our values on a piece of paper. He said, "*Just write down whatever is most important to you, whether it's your relationship with your grandmother, or your health—whatever it is, just write down what's important to you.*" Then he told us to keep that with us in our notebooks and bring it to class everyday, and that was it.

A couple of weeks later, he started a second assignment for us, which was to keep a daily journal. In the morning, we were to write down what we had planned for that day. Then, before we went to bed, we had to take note of what we did and didn't accomplish, assessing what our progress was for the day.

For several weeks, maybe even a few months, we did that every day. Then one day he asked us to bring the journal to school and bring out that piece of paper with our values on it and compare the two. That was the end of the exercise. He didn't give us any lesson that accompanied the exercise: he just left it with us to draw our own conclusions.

For me, that was a profound moment, because I compared the two and there was a huge discrepancy. It was very clear that there were only two options. One was to look in the mirror and face the fact that most people out there, myself included, are lying to themselves. When it comes to those values we say are so important to us, we aren't, in reality, living them or incorporating them into our lives. So you have to admit that you're lying to yourself. That's the first option.

The more difficult option is to change your life, to change your daily actions in a fundamental and radical way that pulls them into the orbit of your values.

I was probably 17 when I had this experience, and for me that was just a game-changer. It wasn't immediate, but I think that really started to change the gears of my mind, in a way.

That also started to correspond with some of the books that he was introducing us to, like *Demian* and *Slaughterhouse Five*, and so forth.

Later on, when I graduated high school, he gave me this beautiful card and the book *The Hitchhiker's Guide to the Galaxy*. In the card he wrote, *I wasn't quite sure what book to give you. I thought of **Siddhartha** by Herman Hesse or **Zen and the Art of Motorcycle Maintenance** by Robert Pirsig, but I settled on this one.*

Now, I don't know why, but even to this day I still haven't read *The Hitchhiker's Guide to the Galaxy*, but I went out and I bought

*Siddhartha* and read it in one night, and it was a very profound experience for me.

I started thinking about what I did on a typical weekday night—watch a sitcom or something—where does that go? I wouldn't even remember the content in a day or two. But that book, those couple of hours, changed me in so many ways that I can't even articulate it.

**HB**: Imagine if you'd actually read *The Hitchhiker's Guide to the Galaxy*. You might be a completely different person than you are today.

**MB**: Maybe I would be. But I started with *Siddhartha*, and then I went to *Zen and the Art of Motorcycle Maintenance*, which was an even more powerful experience for me. I read that just as I was starting college. I started thinking about how these books had such an incredible impact on me, and I was also aware of the fact that at the age of 18 I could only speak English, I had only lived in the United States, I had only seen one side of things. I felt like I had been starved all these years and I needed to catch up, so I just started reading voraciously.

The goal I gave myself was a book a day. Mind you, these weren't Tom Clancy novels. I was reading Plato and *Crime and Punishment* and Walden and all the great philosophy classics of both the classical and modern eras: Kafka, Nietzsche, and Schopenhauer. I remember I read Schopenhauer's *On the Basis of Morality*, and that was another of those profound moments.

I had very little social life that first year in college. I didn't make a lot of friends. I didn't go to parties or anything like that, so there was a big disconnect between my experience and what is generally associated with the freshman year of college. But for me it was this beautiful, wonderful, and exciting intellectual journey. I was reading voraciously. I started taking all these literature and philosophy classes. For that first year that's all I did: just read, read, read.

That's also when I went to the study-abroad office to start looking into opportunities to go abroad. They ended up making an exception for me and let me go to China for my sophomore year when I was 19. Usually they want you to wait until your junior year, but I kept going there and pleading my case, and they eventually let me go.

That first year I went to China, I don't think I read a single book. It was all experience. Those two years of my life were a very interesting contrast: going from the world of reading to the world of experience.

**HB**: So you kept pushing to study abroad, and they finally said, "*Okay, you can go to China.*" Did they allow you to go anywhere and you picked China, or did you just wind up, somewhat randomly, going to China? Once you went there, were you living with a family? How did you learn the language? Did you learn any of it ahead of time?

**MB**: It turned out that there was a consortium that William Paterson was a member of, together with one of the other colleges—I believe it was either the City University of New York, or the State University of New York at Staten Island. They had a brand new program in Nanjing. It was the first semester it had ever run, so I was able to go to Nanjing through that program, through this consortium. Of my shortlist of countries that seemed to be interesting, that was the only one where an opportunity to go existed, so I took it. It was a brand new program, so there were a lot of quirks that were being worked out, but it was life-changing.

**HB**: Language acquisition, cultural acquisition, integration and immersion into society—how did that all happen?

**MB**: Slowly, at first. When I went there I didn't have any previous background in Chinese language. I remember drawing pictures of noodles in restaurants to try to convey what I wanted to order.

At that point, foreign students in China were very much segregated. There was no such thing as living with a Chinese family or having a Chinese roommate. If I remember correctly, in Nanjing (where I was) there was only one program that was given special permission for foreigners to be allocated Chinese roommates: the Johns Hopkins Nanjing Program, of which I was not a part.

I remember lobbying the administration to give me a non-English-speaking roommate—somebody from Southeast Asia or Korea, or Japan, so we would be forced to speak Chinese—but they wouldn't do it. They kept giving me American roommates.

So the second best thing I could do was make my own opportunities. I bought a cheap bicycle and would explore the city every night and every weekend. Nanjing is one of the so-called "ancient capitals" of China, so there's an incredible amount of rich history and culture: old temples, former palaces, all kinds of parks, like the Yuhuatai Martyr's Park in the south of the city. I had a huge map of the city and I would pick a different scenic site and get out there. Sometimes I had to take buses. Other times I would ride my bicycle. I would explore all these different places and I would try to talk to as many people as I could, although I had a limited vocabulary.

**HB**: You must have been taking some kind of formal Chinese language classes at that point though, right?

**MB**: Yes. I had two hours of Chinese class a day, and then another hour or two of content courses like Chinese culture, Chinese geography, and so forth.

**HB**: What year was this, exactly?

**MB**: This was 1993, so just a few years after the Tiananmen Square incident. The engines were revving up for China's economic miracle, but it hadn't quite taken off yet. It was a really interesting time to be in China.

Nanjing was so different from anything I had ever experienced. I was this kid born in the mid-West who grew up in suburban New Jersey, and all of a sudden I was in an environment where the rules were very different.

During that year, a good friend of mine asked me, "*Do you know what the cheapest thing in China is?*" and the answer was "people". There were a lot of very sad circumstances that you would see all the time that would attest to that type of a statement. You would see little kids who didn't have residence permits so they couldn't go to school and didn't have access to hospitals or doctors or anything like that. You'd see kids who were half naked, begging in the street. You're simply not exposed to that sort of thing living in a suburban town in the US.

Naturally, those kinds of experiences had very profound effects on me, let alone the everyday realities and bureaucracies of the system—socialist China, as it was at that period. In China at that time, little things like mailing a letter or getting a student ID card could be much more difficult than you might anticipate. Also, for the first time, I was confronted with my identity in a way that I never had been growing up, say, as a white person in America.

**HB**: Insofar as you were "the other"? Is that what you mean?

**MB**: Yes. You are "the other". You would directly face issues of prejudice. Of course, in America you grow up learning all about race—that's kind of the elephant in the room, and still some people don't like to talk about it. Even now, on the news, you see all kinds of black and white race issues playing out in the US. I always thought I was a pretty sensitive person vis-à-vis race issues, but until you're on the other side of the table, you can't really know what it's like.

For example, going to a public swimming pool and being told that you can't go in because the guy selling tickets is afraid you'll infect everyone with a sexually transmitted disease (because, of course, all foreigners have STDs), or being called "a big white monkey" on the bus— those kinds of things would happen on a daily basis. I had a lot of classmates who got very frustrated with those experiences, but I tried to take it as a learning experience, one that would make me more sensitive to these issues of race and difference.

**HB**: You clearly went in with a very open-minded, passionately-exploratory type of attitude. You were bugging the study-abroad office to be able to participate in this program. You weren't even really very discriminating in terms of where you went at that stage. You were desperately open to new experiences. You seem to be the sort of person who wasn't going to whine and complain and say, "*This* *isn't like home*," because that was exactly what you were trying to get away from. You wanted to expose yourself to these circumstances.

As you said, some of these circumstances were negative, in terms of discrimination and so forth. At the time were you thinking to yourself, *This is a wonderful thing*, or *Chinese culture is great*, or *This place, in some way, resonates with me*? Or were you thinking something more along the lines of, *It's great to be out of New Jersey. Maybe next time I'll go to Indonesia or somewhere else*?

**MB**: I guess the best way to describe it would be that I felt like a sponge: I was insatiable. I felt there was so much out there that I could absorb. There's the old adage, *The more you learn, you realize the less you know*. That was me. First I spent a year reading voraciously, and then I was experiencing all these things in a new place.

That experience of the previous year, with all that reading, paired with the experience of being in China, just made me feel that there was so much out there, and I still felt ignorant of everything. And my Chinese language ability was very weak when I arrived.

**HB**: How long did it take to get some sort of facility with the language—because that's, of course, an integral component of interacting with people, appreciating the culture, and generally understanding what's going on. How hard was that?

**MB**: I recall having a very limited vocabulary for the first six months or so; and I was often too shy to use it when I went out, or people just couldn't understand what I was saying. I would spend a lot of time sitting in my room writing out Chinese characters. They have these little books that elementary-school children use when they're learning to write Chinese. They have what look like tic-tac-toe grids, and you write the characters in the boxes. They're just made for practicing the different characters. I would fill these up. I'm pretty sure, in my garage, I still have dozens and dozens of these books, with hundreds, even thousands, of these characters. You just write them over and over again. That's really the only way to learn, to hammer these characters into your mind—just write them out repeatedly.

So I would write them constantly, and then I would go out and use whatever fragmented piece of the language I could. Then, between six and nine months after arriving, things started to click. I started finding that all that hard work, reviewing grammar exercises and writing characters, started to come together. I felt like I could actually start communicating with people. I stayed there a full year during that first trip. By the time I left, I could have full, pretty decent, basic conversations with people.

Not too long after I returned to New Jersey, I went to our public library and picked up a Chinese novel. I didn't know it at the time, but this was a trashy romance novel, effectively the equivalent of Danielle Steel, or something like that. But the point of the story is that I could read it. I remember thinking how good a feeling that was. That was the first Chinese book I read, and I read it cover to cover and barely needed a dictionary. That was a great sense of empowerment.

I started realizing that it's not that big a leap from working through a textbook with a dictionary to working through the short stories of Lu Xun, the father of modern Chinese literature. So I started giving myself the latter as a challenge.

I started listening to Chinese pop music. Bear in mind that I was someone who had always loved jazz, jazz-fusion, and all kinds of instrumental music, but I started listening to Chinese pop music and reading the lyrics to learn Chinese. It was great for pronunciation. It doesn't help with tones, because the tones fall out when you sing, but for the pronunciation it was great.

That even applied when I started learning traditional Chinese characters, because Chinese pop music, at least at that time—in the early 90s—was imported from Hong Kong and Taiwan, and they were using traditional Chinese characters. So my first encounter with traditional characters, versus simplified ones, was through pop songs on these little cassettes.

**HB**: What's the difference between the traditional and simplified characters?

**MB**: In the People's Republic of China (PRC), there were a lot of policies that were put in place to pull society up and raise the standard of living. One of the policies was to raise literacy.

And one of the ways to raise literacy was to simplify the characters. So a character that had, say, 20 strokes would then be reduced to, say, 8. As a result, there's a whole lexicon of simplified characters that is in common use in the People's Republic of China, whereas in Taiwan and Hong Kong they still use traditional characters.

The stakes for using traditional versus simplified Chinese were quite high, because for many years Taiwan wanted to present itself as the cradle of traditional Chinese culture that carried on the torch of all those great Chinese traditions—Confucianism, religion, and so forth—and one very important aspect of that was preserving the characters. That gave the Taiwanese government the opportunity to say that mainland China was destroying the language by adopting simplified characters, calling it a defilement of the language.

**HB**: Is there anything that's different other than the actual number of strokes used to write them? Does one pronounce anything differently? Does that have any effect on anything other than the way it looks?

**MB**: It's primarily just that the number of strokes is less; but characters are made up of radicals, and radicals do have meaning in and of themselves. And sometimes when a character is simplified, some of the radicals will be taken out.

For example, the traditional version of the character for "love" "*ài*", has a heart radical in the middle, whereas the simplified version doesn't have that heart radical. So when you write the word "love" in Hong Kong or Taiwan there's a physical heart that's embodied in the character, whereas in China that's missing.

愛    爱

Traditional Chinese Character          Simplified Chinese Character

**HB**: So one could say there's a certain sense of nuance that's lost when the character is simplified?

**MB**: Yes, certainly. There is a whole level of meaning that's taken out when reducing the stroke order, because those clusters of strokes make up radicals that do have, sometimes, phonetic meaning, as well as sometimes meaning in terms of the content.

There are also differences in pronunciation in some cases, but that will often be represented by a different character. Take the word "tomato". In mainland China they would typically say "xīhóng-shì", whereas in Taiwan it is called "fānqié". The pronunciation is completely different. They use different characters. "Potato" is another example. A potato is called "tudou" in China and "maling-shu" in Taiwan.'

**HB**: So in a relatively short period of time you're seeing this divergence in the language due to the politics, geography, history, and so forth. And layered on top of that there's all this political posturing: *We're the ones who are carrying the torch* or *We're the ones who are reinventing things in such a way that it directly benefits the people.*

**MB**: Right. Both sides spin the issue: the preservation of traditional Chinese culture being a good thing in Taiwan, the simplification of characters being a greater good to raise literacy in mainland China—which it certainly did.

But besides the politics, there are, of course, also regional differences. There are certain local dialects spoken in Taiwan that aren't spoken in the mainland, or dialects that are only spoken in Hong Kong. Those dialectical issues also influence the written language in different ways as well.

And the histories are different. Even before 1949, Taiwan had a very different history for several hundred years. It was on a different path economically and culturally, so all of that leads to different linguistic associations.

## Questions for Discussion:

*1. Have you been particularly influenced by (at least) one outstanding high school teacher, as Michael clearly was by Mr Jensen?*

*2. To what extent does the university focus on "job-related skills" limit the opportunity for personal development? Should all students be encouraged to take a "study-abroad year" during university?*

*3. Why does Michael say "Even before 1949"? What happened in mainland China and Taiwan in 1949?*

## II. Found in Translation

*Manifesting values and creating impact*

**HB**: I want to get back to this idea of these different regions, specifically Taiwan and Hong Kong, and how that plays out in film, literature, and all sorts of things. But before I do, I want to finish up your story of how you embarked on your subsequent career trajectory.

You came back to the United States after this year abroad. How did that motivate you or move you in a direction where you became very specialized and very knowledgeable about this part of the world?

**MB**: I came back and I wanted to continue building on that foundation that I started. They didn't have a Chinese program at William Paterson College at that time, so I transferred to Rutgers and I ended up getting a fellowship to go to Taiwan for a second full year of study abroad, and that was the year that things really blossomed. My language abilities went from being able to read a basic novel with the help of a dictionary to reading novels quite frequently, going to lectures, and just sucking the marrow out of that experience as much as I could.

Whereas during my first year in Nanjing I was going to temples and touristy places, in Taiwan I was going to lectures and auditing classes at different universities. It was a different level of access to the culture and engagement with what was happening around me.

When I came back after that year and was finishing up at Rutgers, getting closer to graduating, I began wondering, *Where do I go next?*

One thing I had done during my senior year in college was translate a short article for one of my professors to be published in an academic journal, and I really enjoyed that experience. As I was thinking about what to do during the summer after graduating, I thought that maybe I could get a job as a waiter (as I had done in high school), or I could try to do something more meaningful with these skills that I had worked so hard to develop.

And I thought, *Why not translate a novel?* There was a novel I had read in Taiwan called *To Live* by Yu Hua, and there was also a film that had been made by Zhang Yimou, probably China's best known director. I sent a fax to Yu Hua—this was at a time when people still sent faxes (I got his contact information from one of my professors)—and he agreed.

**HB**: As you say, this was a very successful novel. No one had thought of translating it into English before that point?

**MB**: No. This was before there was a huge appetite for Chinese fiction in the West. But he gave me the rights, and so I translated it that summer. It was done in a couple of months. But it sat in my drawer for years before a publisher would finally publish it. It wasn't published until around 2003 or 2004.

**HB**: So you just contacted the author directly? That's great.

**MB**: That has actually continued to be my pattern for literary translations. I still haven't translated a novel that I was commissioned to do. It always starts with me falling in love with a book and then contacting the writer and getting permission to do it.

**HB**: That experience, when you were engaged in that translation— tell me about how it made you feel, not only in terms of your grasp of Chinese, but also your appreciation of English. Because this is an interesting mindset that one gets in when one starts playing around with these things.

**MB**: Oh, yes. A lot of people say that there's no better form of close reading than translation, because you're really mulling over every nuance of every word—at least I do. There are a lot of technical translators who are working per word, or per hour, and as a result they are just pumping things out. But for what I was doing, the stakes were very high—perhaps even higher than they should have been, I don't know. I took it very seriously. I invested a lot of thought into the correct rendering of every word.

One thing about translating from Chinese to English—as opposed to, say, French to English, or Spanish to English—is that, because English has certain common linguistic roots with a number of other Western languages, there is going to be a natural equivalent for certain terms. So, say, "sadness" in one of these languages is likely going to have a roughly equivalent term—it may even sound almost identical.

But in Chinese, the term "bēishāng" could also mean melancholic, depressed, mournful—a lot of different things, depending entirely on context. That means that the translator has a lot more leeway and wiggle room, but also a lot more responsibility to find, in that context, what the Chinese word really means. In that sense, you have a little bit more creative freedom, but you also have to give it a lot more thought.

**HB**: And there's more responsibility, presumably.

**MB**: Yes. When I'm translating dialogue, for example, I'll often speak aloud just to double-check whether people actually talk like that in English, and try to figure out what the perfect equivalent is for capturing the nuance of the original. I think that you have to have a sensitivity of both languages to really capture how someone would express that idea, or thought, or emotion, in the other language. I think that's key to being successful as a translator.

A lot of people talk about "faithful" translations or "literal" translations. Often, to create the most faithful translation you have to betray the literal meaning in order to get at that faithful spirit. In Chinese, for example, a very common greeting that people will say to each other is literally, *"Have you eaten?"* But you wouldn't say that in a Western country. If I saw you on the street, I wouldn't say, *"Howard, have you eaten?"* It would sound very weird. A far better translation would be something like, *"How's it going?"* because you want to capture that spirit. They weren't actually asking if you had eaten. It's just a greeting.

**HB**: Sure. The intentionality is what you're looking for.

**MB**: Right. You always have to constantly navigate between being faithful to the original and making it readable. That's the tightrope that you're always walking as a translator: between faithfulness to the original and readability to your target audience. Some translators are more on one side than the other. There's no one answer to this.

I don't have a lot of macro-theories that dominate my work as a translator. It's more of a gut feeling, an aesthetic, for what sounds good and what sounds right in that language and for that particular work.

All of the novels I've translated have been in very different registers, ranging from historical novels to contemporary ones: I did one about teenage punks in Taiwan, for example (*Wild Kids* by Ta-chun Chang). Different linguistic registers require a different approach, a different aesthetic; and what works in one universe is not necessarily going to work in the other.

**HB**: As you just told me, you're not commissioned to do translations, so when you decide to take on a project, you first have to be personally engaged with the work. What is that driven by? Is it that you really enjoy the book and you believe it should have a wider readership, or is it that you want to challenge yourself in a different style? What's going through your mind at that time?

**MB**: It's a combination of things. At the heart of it is this almost primal urge: *I need to translate this book.* I just feel such a connection with the work, and am overwhelmed with its power and impact: it's definitely a very emotional experience. Then there's the sense—at least for most of the translations I've worked on—that, in one sense or another, it was a contemporary classic, or perhaps had the potential to be a classic. It's a work that is going to stand the test of time, already receiving a certain degree of attention and readership in the

Chinese market, a work that had resonated with Chinese readers in a way that I believe could cross boundaries and also resonate with international readers. In short, it would be meaningful, in a way that goes back to what I was talking about earlier. It seemed more meaningful to do these translations than not to do them. I had the skills and I had the time.

This is backtracking a little bit to Mr Jensen and making that choice to change your life and live in accordance with your values. If you really make the effort, the result can be that, when you look back in a decade or two—or three or four—there's some kind of structure and beauty. There's something left behind there.

A good metaphor is that when my students write essays, they start with an outline. We often recommend that they do that to ensure that they have a good structure. But how many of us actually do outlines for our lives? I think a lot of people just go from job to job, living day to day and seeing what's next, but they don't really have a plan.

That's not to say that I have some grand plan for my life, but it became clear to me that I should try to make choices such that I can use my time in a way that I'm making quality decisions that are going to lead towards leaving something behind. Sometimes I even wonder, *Who reads these books anyway?* Often very few people do, but it seems that, in the lesser of two evils of this kind of existential quandary that we all face, the better choice is to try to do something that's going to leave something behind.

For me—especially at that stage of my life when I was quite young, in my grad student years—choosing to translate those novels was the best choice. It seemed to me that I could just do typical grad student stuff—going to classes, writing papers, and everything else —or I could take a couple hours a day and produce these translations of masterpieces of modern Chinese literature.

I think a lot of my translations were driven by an attempt to manifest some of those values, trying to leave something behind that could hopefully make an impact on someone.

**HB**: I had the pleasure of talking to another translator some time ago, David Bellos (*Babbling Barbarians: How Translators Keep Us Civilized*), who wrote a book called *Is That A Fish in Your Ear? Translation and the Meaning of Everything*. He's the director of the Translation Studies program at Princeton. You also teach translation, right?

**MB**: That's right. I do.

**HB**: So there's being a translator, but there's also communicating the act of translating.

Is That A Fish in Your Ear? had all these little vignettes about the art of translation—what translation is, what it is not, and so forth. And I remember that something that stuck in his craw was the notion that a translation is never the same as the original, the pejorative way that some people say, "*Well, that's just a translation. You should read it in the original.*" Of course, it's impossible for most people to read everything in the original, in every language, all the time.

But there is also this notion of the translator being creative himself or herself. You mentioned before that there's a sense of responsibility, as well as a sense of creativity. When you're teaching translation, what sorts of things do you advise your students to do?

**MB**: One thing I recommend is that they need to have a very solid foundation in both languages (at least two). That's not something you can do in a short time-span. Either you already have it, or you don't and you slowly work towards it.

You also need to have a certain sensitivity towards language. Ideally, you should be well-read in both languages. I think one trap a lot of people in my field fall into is that they read all this Chinese work, but then they fall behind on what's happening in English literature. You really need to somehow keep a foot in both worlds, because you also need to keep up on your target language and make sure that your written English is at a certain level and has a certain literary weight to it that's going to compliment and be able to rise up to the level of that original.

There's no simple shortcut for teaching translation. The way I usually teach it is in a workshop style. We'll start off reading different translations of a single text. I'll give the students one short story in Chinese along with, say, four or five different English translations of the same story. Then we'll go through each one and analyze the different decisions that were made by the translator and talk about the pros and cons of these different strategies.

Slowly I start easing them into doing translation on their own. We'll workshop it. They'll read each other's work and critique it.

The only way to do it is to do it. The more experience you have, hopefully, the better you'll get. You really have to jump in and get your hands dirty, and you can't be afraid to make mistakes. The great thing about the computer age is that revising is quite easily done now. When I first started we had word processors, which were basically like typewriters. Now there's a lot more freedom in terms of revisiting translations, tweaking them, and going through them version after version.

## Questions for Discussion:

*1. Should all translators share the sort of emotional bond with the work that they are translating that Michael describes in this chapter?*

*2. Do you agree that a translation is "never the same as the original"? Should a translator be regarded as an author himself or herself when it comes to the text in question?*

## III. Freedom of the Press

*Rewriting novels and denying translations*

**HB**: Excluding yourself for the moment, do you think it's a meaningful statement to say that there are better and worse translators?

**MB**: Of course there are a few translations out there that a mass of critics would probably agree are fairly poorly done, and there are a lot that were done very well. If you look at the market of Chinese-language fiction, I wouldn't say there's a monopoly, but the field has been dominated over the last several decades by one individual: Howard Goldblatt.

He used to teach at the University of Colorado Boulder and then went on to be a research professor at Notre Dame. He has single-handedly translated upwards of 40 novels from Chinese into English, and he's still as prolific as ever. If you were to randomly pick up a contemporary Chinese novel in translation, chances are that he's the translator. His contributions to this field have been immense. He's an incredible translator.

The one criticism you'll sometimes hear about his works would be that there are certain rewrites or deletions of certain passages, paragraphs, or chapters that he's done—in most cases with the author's permission—often at the request of various publishers.

For example, he's the translator of Mo Yan—the Nobel Prize-winning writer—and in a few of his novels the US publisher wasn't happy with a certain conclusion or certain section. So Goldblatt then went to Mo Yan and told him that the publisher wasn't happy with a certain part of the book; and in some cases Mo Yan produced a whole new conclusion to a book, which is what ended up getting translated.

**HB**: Hold on. Hold on. I need to wrap my head around this. We have a book that an author has written, a completed work, which was generally well received. And then the publisher says to the translator, *"We don't like the way this book ends. Go back to the writer and get a new ending."* That's what's happening?

**MB**: Yes.

**HB**: That's crazy.

**MB**: Well, it does speak to a certain set of expectations on the part of American publishers.

**HB**: I'll say.

**MB**: Although the work is published in Chinese, for the American market they probably see it as a new work that's still open to molding and revision.

**HB**: Is this just an American thing? Do the British do it too? Is this essentially an Anglosphere phenomenon? Do Australian publishers say, *"Please rewrite the middle chapters because there's no kangaroo in there"*?

**MB**: I think it's primarily American publishers that have done this. My sense of it—trying to step back to be a little more fair-minded—

**HB**: I'm being perfectly fair-minded. They're just wrong, that's all.

**MB**: Well, if I try to put myself in their shoes, I think it's that they're used to working with writers where there's a very close, almost collaborative, relationship between the editor and the writer, where there's a lot of give and take, and exchange. You can find all kinds of interviews and discussions about this online. There's quite a lot of talk about these kinds of issues. It doesn't happen with every book, but there are several examples where this has happened.

**HB**: Has this happened to you? Have you been asked to go back to the writer and have him turn it upside down because, in the publisher's view, the conclusion wouldn't suit the American public?

**MB**: I've worked primarily with university presses, which are better at respecting the intentionality of the original work, and I've had a very good relationship with the university presses I've worked with. I've worked with a few commercial presses where there was a little bit of that—not on a macro-level, like rewriting the ending, or a new introduction, or something like that—but there were times working with publishers where there were subtle language issues, where the editor would change something in a way that I felt was pulling us away from the original and too far towards pleasing the readers.

So when I'd get the galley proofs, I'd change it back; and then when they sent it back to me a second time they would change it back again, and we'd have this little tug-of-war. But in those cases it was a word here or a sentence there. It wasn't the entire ending or something like that.

I have had recommendations for more radical changes. One of the more notable ones concerned this novel I translated called *The Song of Everlasting Sorrow* by Wang Anyi, who is generally regarded as one of the greatest living writers in China. She's produced an incredible volume of work. She's won basically every major literary award in China. This novel in particular had received the Mao Dun Prize, which is basically China's top literary prize.

It's a novel that spans four decades in the life of a woman from Shanghai, and the fate of the city somehow parallels her life. It begins with about 40 pages of essayistic descriptions of the alleys and the pigeons and the architecture of the city, and it's only after that preamble that the female protagonist enters.

I did have one publisher recommend that I just cut out that entire 40-page section. Another recommended that I change the title to *Shanghai Girl* instead of *The Song of Everlasting Sorrow*—that was a few years after a very popular novel called *Shanghai Baby* was published.

Those were somewhat off-putting experiences, I have to say. And in the end, I went with Columbia University Press, which respected the original vision of the work, so nothing was cut. But there definitely were those sorts of requests: *This novel would do a lot better if you'd just cut those forty pages.*

**HB**: Well, that's just appalling. Maybe I'm just a purist, and not as fair-minded as I should be and so forth, but I'm having a hard time understanding why in God's name they would be putting pressure on you to change even one word.

If I'm the editor at some publishing house and you're the translator, and there's a writer out there somewhere, what business is it of mine to be telling you that you should be changing even *one word*? Unless there's a sense that you don't have a sufficient command of English idiom or something—in which case, why on earth have I agreed for you to be the translator in the first place? The whole idea of an editor saying, "*You should really change this word over here*," just doesn't make any sense to me at all.

**MB**: I've certainly worked with a lot of editors where I can fairly say that they helped raise the book to another level in certain ways— they've made a substantial contribution to that book in terms of tweaking, or polishing, or word choice, and all the wonderful things editors do. It's a fine line between editing a work and then starting to make changes that actually result in the content being affected. Where that line is, is hazy.

The same editor who, in some cases, crossed the line, in other cases, might have made suggestions that I thought did make sense, and which I liked more than what I had originally done. In other cases it's different. In almost all cases, the editors do not speak Chinese, so they're basing all of these editorial changes on what they see in black and white on that page in English, whereas the translator has this other text that he or she can reference.

**HB**: Right. **The** text. The *actual, original* text. Of the writer.

**MB**: Yes. And in some cases, the changes are still within the realm of—for me, at least—what's acceptable; and in some cases are even better than what I originally did. But in other cases, because they don't have that road map, they might try to take the work in another direction. That's where I sometimes have a difference of opinion with an editor.

Often when you read—whether it's a translation scholar, literary critics, or even just book reviewers—they'll talk about the writer and they'll talk about the translator. If the novel is a masterpiece, the author is brilliant. But if they don't like it, then it's a terrible translation. You often get that sort of dynamic going on. But the missing component is the editor. Nobody ever talks about the editors and their role in the middle.

Regarding Howard Goldblatt, whom I mentioned earlier—there's a lot of criticism that comes up here and there about those changes to the text, but most of it is directed at him. I want to stress that nobody has done as much for Chinese literature in English translation as he has. But at the same time, nobody takes into consideration the role of these editors at publishing houses who are pushing in a certain direction—and, in most cases, the authors are agreeing to the changes as well.

When you read the translation, you never know what is coming from the original and is representing that spirit, what's representing the vision of the translator, and—the mystery factor—what's coming from the editor. You don't know how many of those words are coming out of the mouths of these editors.

That's something that, when we're reading and critiquing literature, we should always think about: that it's not just between the author and the audience, or the author and the translator, but also involves the editors and that crucial role they play in the middle. Sometimes it's positive, and sometimes it can alter things in ways that take us a little further away from the original.

**HB**: I recognize that in any dynamic you can have positive change. If an editor says that you need to move it in one direction or another, for example, I can see how that might be helpful. But that's a dialogue: *Well, Michael, have you thought about changing it this way or that way to improve the flow*? That's a very different process, it seems to me than saying that you should change the title or the ending or even randomly take out specific words.

And my sense is—not wanting to sound like some radical, anti-capitalist or anything, as nothing could be further from the truth given my current line of work—that academic presses would generally be much more inclined towards preserving the fundamental intentionality that I, as a reader, am interested in extracting.

**MB**: Right. Well, there are certain things that some commercial presses do that might speak to some of your sentiments. For example, academic presses that I work with will put the translator's name on the book, while commercial presses will usually fight against that. The rationale is that Americans don't read literature in translation, so putting on the cover, *Translated by so-and-so* is just going to turn them away.

**HB**: They want to hide the fact that the book wasn't actually written in English to start with?

**MB**: Most commercial presses are resistant to putting a translator's name on the cover. My response to that, and my general feeling, is that it's a chicken-and-egg situation. Their take is that Americans don't read translations, so maybe they should downplay that.

**HB**: Exactly. Maybe they don't read translations because they don't get exposed to translations.

**MB**: Right. But publishers already have this preconceived notion that Americans don't read translations, so they're not going to publish as many, or push them, or market them, in the same way that they would an English novel.

**HB**: Don't get me started.

**MB**: Well, I think back to the Mr Jensen days in high school when I read *Demian* by Herman Hesse. Did I even *know* that was a translation? I don't think I did. Did I *care* that it was a translation? Did I care who the translator was? No. It was just a work of great literature.

## Questions for Discussion:

*1. Do you think that more Americans would opt for translated literature if given the opportunity?*

*2. Why do you think that some countries are more open to translated literature than others? Which countries would you guess would be the most open? The least?*

# IV. Contemporary Voices

*Literature, film, soft power, and cultural imbalances*

**HB**: The good news seems to be that things are moving—slowly, but inevitably—in the right direction. Perhaps it's because China is becoming more recognized as an economic power—as a country one has to deal with whether one likes it or not—it's impinging itself on the public consciousness to the extent that it's no longer considered eccentric to be interested in what's happening in China. And what's happening in China is, of course, represented in some ways at least, by its literature and films.

Let's talk about some of these cultural aspects: how they've changed in the past and how they're changing now.

I've read one work of contemporary Chinese literature recently, one that you mentioned earlier having launched you into translation: *To Live*, by Yu Hua. I thought it was very moving and interesting. It was not the most uplifting book I've ever read, but it was certainly a powerful piece of literature that I quite enjoyed.

What would your recommendations be, in terms of what I should be reading now, as somebody who knows very little about Chinese literature?

**MB**: I think the contemporary Chinese literary scene is very exciting and very diverse. There have been a lot of incredible voices coming out of China over the last couple of decades.

I would recommend some works by Mo Yan, who was translated by Howard Goldblatt, as I mentioned. Mo Yan has a very vivid imagination, he's an incredible writer. There is certainly an influence of Latin American magical realism that you can sense in his work, but also a scathing allegorical vision of what contemporary China is and what modern Chinese history is. His novel *The Republic of Wine* is a masterpiece.

**HB**: So there is some clear social criticism as well?

**MB**: Oh, certainly. There are a lot of novelists who have produced works that are just as scathing as anything Orwell ever wrote. A lot of people talk about the censorship in China—it's there, of course—but there's still quite a lot of room in today's China, especially in literature (more so than in film), to publish rather explosive works. Of course, if it's too explosive, it's going to be suppressed.

Mo Yan is one example. Yan Lianke is another. He's an incredible writer who is basically a contemporary of Mo Yan, but he's only begun to get serious recognition over the last decade or so. He has a new novel called *The Chronicles of Zhalie*, which is also an allegorical novel. Zhalie is a fictional town, and the name means "to explode", so it's like a chronicle of explosion, with "explosion", in this sense, being a metaphor for China's development. It traces the course of about 30–40 years—the Reform Era from the late '70s, early '80s, to the present—in a little farm town with a population of less than 100 people, and how it slowly evolved from a little village, to a town, to a city, and then eventually to a super-city. It carries out this incredible transformation.

It starts with the men looting the trains that pass nearby, and the women going into the "entertainment" industry—the sex industry—basically using their bodies as capital. Through the women selling themselves and the men selling their labour, they build this city up in a very visceral, brutal way. It's mired in corruption and filth and all kinds of crazy stories. Finally the city evolves into a super-city that is gearing up for the next World War with America. It's a fantastically wild and incredibly imaginative novel.

**HB**: That's a very strong social indictment. Is that fairly typical of the contemporary cutting-edge literary scene? To some extent, you would expect that. This is a society going through tumultuous changes; and whenever that happens, you have the artists who are at the vanguard of criticism and commentary—the writers, the filmmakers, the thinkers and so forth. So what you've said is not terribly surprising, yet it does jar a bit with the image of China that I certainly have, which is that dissent is quickly suppressed.

**MB**: Certain voices of dissent are suppressed, especially when it comes to certain topics: the Tiananmen Square Massacre of 1989, the Uyghur movement in northwest China, Tibetan independence issues, certain aspects of the Cultural Revolution. If you try to publish a book on some of those topics, you can pretty much count on it being banned or suppressed.

But before you talk about what's banned in China, you have to talk about self-censorship in China. Where I live out here in California, near the ocean, there's somebody who has a herd of sheep; and they have an electronic fence that they've put up so the sheep can graze. The sheep, after getting zapped a couple times, don't go anywhere near the fence. They know where it is and they stay pretty far away from it.

In China, there are certain rules for whatever industry you're in, and the cultural industry is no exception to that. Publishers, writers, filmmakers—they all know where those electric fences are, more or less. They're a little less clearly defined than the ones those sheep have, because they sometimes move a little bit, but they are there, and most people just stay away from the fence.

That means that even before the so-called censors or editors tell you to delete something, or that you can't publish it, most authors have already exercised a good degree of self-censorship. The scary product of that is, after so many decades, self-censorship is so internalized and ingrained that it becomes hard to articulate what self-censorship is and what's just a way of life.

**HB**: Or even worse, when you never even think about these kinds of things at all.

**MB**: Exactly. So that's certainly a big component of how the cultural industry works in China.

**HB**: Is it loosening, though? If one were to plot where the fences are, as it were, can one say, albeit with some generality, that the fences are being pushed back? If you look at where those fences were 25 years ago, has there been any change?

**MB**: Yes. If I were to look back 25 years, I would say that the fences have definitely been pushed out, so there's more freedom now, in some ways.

In other ways, the authorities have become more sensitive and concerned about certain topics, which a lot of people might not have imagined they would.

For example, the 11th Annual Beijing Independent Film Festival was set to be held in Songzhuang. On the opening day of the previous year's event—the 10th annual festival—the authorities came and shut off the power, effectively shutting down the festival.

So the following year, in 2014, the festival poster was a picture of a power generator, because they bought a portable power generator in case that happened again. Well, the morning of—or maybe it was the night before—the film festival was set to open, the authorities came and confiscated the power generator and shut it down.

Those kinds of things are still happening, but at the same time, the government in China has implemented a new policy within the last year and a half or so about sending Chinese culture out into the world, which has led to incredible state-sponsorship of various cultural enterprises to get Chinese culture out there. It's really a means of using soft power to export Chinese culture to the world and affect political change, economic change, and so forth.

**HB**: It also allows them a chance to indulge in a bit of pride on cultural grounds, which is quite different than the image of China elsewhere as simply a military or economic threat.

**MB**: Exactly. This notion of soft power has been manifested in the establishment of Confucius Institutes all over the world. The subsidizing of translations is an example of this. Just a few years ago, the Chinese Writers Association and the Chinese Ministry of Culture all started setting up very generous translation grants and prizes, basically methods that allow international Sinologists to apply for subsidies and funding to do literary translations.

There are also all kinds of things happening in the Chinese film industry. For example, Wanda is a mega conglomerate in China that owns real estate and used to have ties to the PLA (People's Liberation Army). A few years ago, they bought the AMC movie theater chain.

In the fall of 2013, they had a major press event in Qingdao, China. They flew in Brad Pitt, Angelina Jolie, and many A-listers from Hollywood to announce the imminent founding of the Wanda-Qingdao Oriental Movie Metropolis, which is scheduled to be the largest film production studio in the world when it's completed. I've read different things, but the estimated budget to build this thing is somewhere between $4.5 and $6.5 billion.

**HB**: Wow. This is all state-controlled? How does that work?

**MB**: It's not all state-controlled anymore. From the '40s all the way through the early '80s, there were a number of state-owned film studios: the Beijing Film Studio, Changchun Film Studio, Shanghai Film Studio, and so forth. Any film you ever saw in China would say "produced by" one of those studios, sometimes two.

If you look at the credits of a typical film being made in China today, the producer credits will include a list of maybe 6–12 different production companies. Some of them are privately-owned, some have ties to the state, some are based in Hong Kong, some are multinational companies.

But just looking at that difference in the film credits from, say, a 1981 film to something made today, illustrates a very visceral, radical shift in terms of privatization and this capitalist behemoth that's rising up in all sectors of Chinese society.

Some people still cling to the notion that China is associated with socialism or communism, and technically the government still clings to those concepts, but in effect those are long dead and the capitalist spirit of China is more fervent than anything you'd find in America, or anywhere else.

The film industry is very much benefiting from this move towards soft power, and you're seeing more Chinese films being distributed internationally. There are a lot of changes happening on the cultural front. What's interesting is that it's kind of like David vs. Goliath. On the one hand, the state-sanctioned or state-approved cultural products that are deemed worthy are getting all kinds of incredible support, whereas things like this underground film festival are just being squashed.

My feeling is always that, for a healthy cultural scene, whether it's film or literature, you need different voices and different paths. You can't just have the Hollywood blockbuster path. You have to have those independent visions. The sad thing about what's happening in China is that right now the Goliaths are dominating and all those little guys are being shut down.

**HB**: I want to get back to film because there's so much to say about it, but before I do, let me just ask you another question about contemporary Chinese literature.

Given that there are so many more translators of Chinese books and so forth, you might think that a Chinese novelist today would be in a situation where he or she has a much greater likelihood of reaching a global audience. Is that somehow affecting the writing itself in any way that you can see?

**MB**: I think there are quite a few writers in China today who are writing with that global audience in mind. I've had writers approach me wanting me to translate their work—I had one writer whose goal was to get one of her short stories in *The New Yorker*. That was her declared goal. She told me, "*If you get this into The New Yorker, I will buy you a round trip ticket to China,*" and she listed all of the other things she was going to do for me and how much she was going to pay me if I was able to do that. That's an example of somebody who's very goal-oriented and very much aware of that particular niche market—in her eyes, at least, that's the mark of success.

**HB**: Did you get it in *The New Yorker*?

**MB**: Well, I said no.

A few months ago I was on a jury for a literary prize called *The Dream of the Red Chamber Award*, which is awarded every two years in Hong Kong for the best work of full-length Chinese fiction, no matter where the writer is from. I'm not going to reveal any names, but there were some jurors who were criticizing one of the nominees as somebody who "writes for a foreign audience".

So there's still that notion that this writer is pandering to westerners, or "selling out", or what have you.

A lot of people still carry with them the notion that there's a right way to read a novel and a wrong way. Everybody—whether it's a film or a novel—brings with them their own personal baggage and experience, their own tint of rose-coloured glasses that they're wearing. There's no pure way to approach anything. To me, that's what makes life interesting; and that's what makes these readings different.

**HB**: You mentioned people who write in Chinese outside of China. Is there a sense that this Chinese diaspora has a certain style or orientation? And by "outside of China" I don't just mean Taiwan and Hong Kong. I mean potentially much further afield. Can one make generalizations about that sort of literature?

**MB**: People certainly make generalizations all the time, and some of them have a certain weight, I suppose. There are certain sensibilities, say, in Taiwan literature that are different from PRC (People's Republic of China) literature. I don't like broad sweeping statements, but to a certain degree that's true.

**HB**: What would some of those characteristics be?

**MB**: Each region—whether it's Taiwan, Hong Kong, or the PRC— some will say it's all China, but if you look at the reality each one has a very different political, economic, and historical tradition, so the literature is naturally going to reflect that and be affected by that.

For example, in Taiwan in 1947, there was the February 28th Incident, which was a terrible, violent conflict between the nationalist regime and local native Taiwanese. That was a primal scene for so many in Taiwan, and it had an incredible impact on literature and film. Whether directly or indirectly, it left that kind of a historical scar.

Furthermore, Hong Kong and Taiwan were both part of the "Four Little Dragons" that were rising up in the '70s and '80s as the economic miracles of East Asia. That's all going to be reflected in literature and film, and that's going to create a completely different sensibility, aesthetic, and different genres as well.

For instance, the martial arts genre thrived in Hong Kong and Taiwan during the '60s and '70s, whereas in the PRC it was banned. So there are even generic differences in terms of what is popular and prevalent in one Chinese-speaking region versus another one, due to the political circumstances.

Today, of course, we're somewhat past that Cold War moment where you had socialist realism happening in China with all its propagandistic messages, and you had the martial arts escapism fantasy in Hong Kong. But still, those historical roots go pretty deep.

We are in this sort of global Chinese moment where the lines have become more porous and much easier to pass through. If you're in the PRC, say, you can now get tourist visas to go to Taiwan. Since 1997, Hong Kong has been unified with mainland China. If you look at the cultural industries, like the film industry, so many Taiwan and Hong Kong filmmakers are all eking out a living in mainland China because that's where the market is, that's where the money is. If you look at a typical PRC TV miniseries, it's filled with Hong Kong and Taiwan actors. They're all integrated now.

But, that integration aside, there are certain, different, historical paths that they've each taken, and that creates a somewhat different aesthetic, identity, and sensibility for each of those different regions.

Then there are people who are kind of in the middle. There are a lot of writers who are writing in Chinese but are based in America, Canada, Southeast Asia, and so on. There's a group of Chinese Malay writers—some based in Taiwan, some based in other places—who are writing about a very different Chinese experience from their childhood in Malaysia. It's a very diverse cultural scene when you bring it all together.

## Questions for Discussion:

*1. Have you read any contemporary Chinese literature? Has reading this chapter encouraged you to do so? Which of the books explicitly mentioned by Michael is the most interesting to you?*

*2. Do you think that future successes of the Chinese cultural industries will have a positive, negative, or no impact on human rights in China?*

# V. A Glimpse Behind the Lens

*Chinese cinema and cinematographers*

**HB**: I'd like to focus a little more strongly on film now. You've written quite a bit about film and you've conducted many interviews with many very famous Chinese filmmakers that were published as the book *Speaking in Images: Interviews with Contemporary Chinese Filmmakers.*

We don't have to go all the way back, but I'm curious how you became interested in that. Was this a natural by-product of looking at things culturally, or politically, looking at film as a mode of expression in a culture that you were becoming increasingly familiar with and curious about? Or was film, in and of itself, always a real passion of yours?

**MB**: You could say that my interest in film was a structural result of the program I was in for my doctoral studies. At Columbia, where I did my PhD, you had to have three fields. My primary field was modern Chinese literature but the department also encouraged you to go outside the department and take classes. I started taking classes in the film department, and film studies became my second field.

I was very fortunate to have some great teachers like Richard Peña, who was the former director of the New York Film Festival, and James Schamus who was Ang Lee's producer and screenwriter for most of his films—he's now the CEO of Focus Features. After the success of *Crouching Tiger, Hidden Dragon* he went on to do all sorts of great things. I was very fortunate to be able to take classes with them and work with them a little bit, and that fuelled this passion for film.

Another really important part of it was that I was in New York, so there were a lot of people coming and going. When these Chinese filmmakers would come through for the New York Film Festival or the Tribeca Film Festival or just to give a lecture at Columbia, I was often asked to be the interpreter for a lot of these filmmakers because of my language skills. After regularly interpreting for the likes of Zhang Yimou, Zhang Ziyi and Wang Xiaoshuai, you start getting a peek at the other side of the camera. It's not quite the same as working in the industry, but you get a bit of that insider's perspective nonetheless.

**HB**: And you're making personal connections too.

**MB**: Yes. In fact, *Speaking in Images*, the book of interviews that I did, partly resulted from working with these directors on such an extensive basis and seeing what kinds of questions most interviewers were asking.

Most of them were just press interviews; and press interviews are always "timely interviews", which means that they just want a sound bite or a little clip they can use. "*What are you doing next?*" or "*Who's starring in this?*" And those questions don't stand the test of time. They're disposable.

Sometimes we would do a two-day press junket where we would do upwards of 30 interviews. Basically every person was asking them the same questions, and they're all garbage questions. I thought, *Here I am, I've got the language skills and a background in literature and film, and I know all this guy's work*. It just occurred to me how much I could do during two hours with this guy compared to what all those other interviewers were doing. And I had the access because, when you're interpreting, you build up a sense of trust: you become that person's outlet to the world.

So I started doing interviews with some of the directors that I worked with. I published a couple. For me, it was almost an oral history: I wanted to go deep and broad, as opposed to shallow, thin, and disposable.

I wanted to do something that, even in 10 years, when the question, *What's your next film going to be?* isn't going to mean anything, the content would still matter because we're talking about things that are beyond what's happening right now. We're talking about what formed them as film directors, or their aesthetic values, or their upbringing, or a close analysis of some of the films and why they were important.

**HB**: I'm sure they were delighted to have the opportunity to talk to you about it. Everyone wants the opportunity to talk about her work with somebody who is sympathetic, and knowledgeable, and can explore things.

**MB**: Yes, exactly. I think I ended up interviewing 20 filmmakers over the course of a couple years; and that ended up being one of my early book projects, *Speaking in Images*.

**HB**: There's obviously a tremendous amount of wealth, depth, and sensitivity in these interviews that you've conducted. But I was also amazed to discover, when I looked at the foreword by Martin Scorsese, the amount of influence that these films had on people like him. He talks about *The Horse Thief* as his most favourite film from the 1990s and the effect that Fifth Generation filmmakers had on him.

One starts getting this sense of a global community of artists and the influence they're having on one another in a way that I certainly hadn't appreciated. Maybe Scorsese is unique in that respect, but clearly the level of interaction that's happening—presumably in both directions—is becoming increasingly complex and increasingly productive.

**MB**: I think Scorsese *is* unique in the sense that, besides being a filmmaker, he's a film preservationist: he's curated all kinds of film festivals and he has his own personal film archive in New York. He's done several documentaries on the history of film: one on American cinema, another on Italian cinema.

But a more general aspect for any filmmaker is to go to festivals. And at these international film festivals they are exposed to all these other international voices from world cinema. As a result, your typical filmmaker is going to have more of that contact and more of those interactions than the average person would.

**HB**: I'd like you to give me a little bit of an overview of the history of Chinese film. These guys who came along in the early '80s, as I understand it, were considered "the Fifth Generation". Where did that term come from? Maybe that's a good place to start.

**MB**: Fifth Generation filmmakers were the global face of Chinese cinema in the 1980s, when they burst onto the scene. A better description would probably be to call it "Chinese New Wave", because that's basically what it was. Think of the French New Wave or Italian Neorealism: in film history there have always been these movements that have arisen and shaken things up.

There are different explanations for how they got the moniker "the Fifth Generation", but the most typical one is that they were the fifth generation of the graduating class of the Beijing Film Academy, which was the primary training ground for Chinese filmmakers. If you trace back generationally, the First Generation would actually have predated the Beijing Film Academy—but at any rate, that set Chinese film history on this course where groups are looked at generationally.

After the Fifth Generation, the Sixth Generation emerged in the early '90s. Nobody talks about a Seventh Generation because the whole generational division has somewhat lost its teeth. I don't know how useful it is anyway, as a category, calling it "the Fifth Generation". But the main point is that this was the first group of graduates of the Beijing Film Academy post-Cultural Revolution, and that's important for two reasons.

The first is that this group of young graduates had a personal history of experiencing not just the Cultural Revolution, but most of the tumultuous political movements of modern China, from the Anti-Rightist Movement to The Great Leap Forward. Most of them were growing up while all of that was playing out, and most of them went through their formative years during the Cultural Revolution, which had a huge impact on them. That's very much reflected in their work.

At the same time, this is also the same generation that's coming of age and going to university in the Age of Reform and the Open Door Policy, which began around 1978. During the socialist period, China's doors had been primarily closed except to other socialist nations—Albania, the Soviet Union and so forth.

In the West, there was a certain, chronological development to culture, say, from the '50s all the way up to the '80s. Take rock & roll. You've got Buddy Holly, then Chuck Berry, then The Rolling Stones, and then Deep Purple: it changes over time. That was all closed to China. So in the '80s when those doors opened up, they had all of it coming in at the same time: Guns N' Roses, Metallica, Deep Purple, Buddy Holly, Kenny G, Lionel Richie, and Wham! all just thrown at you together. And that was just music.

Now, think of philosophy. All of a sudden these philosophical works that were unavailable during the socialist period came flooding in. If you went into a Chinese bookstore in the '80s you'd suddenly find Nietzsche and Kierkegaard and Freud. Basically, all of these ideas just began exploding at that time in China.

As with philosophy and music, all of this Western film that had been closed off also came flooding in. This Fifth Generation has this very visceral, and in some cases disturbing, experience that they went through during the Cultural Revolution; and then the doors open up and they're exposed to all these incredible new ideas. It's like a cultural renaissance.

**HB**: On amphetamines.

**MB**: Exactly. It's hard to capture how exciting that period must have been. A whole series of native Chinese cultural movements started emerging in different media. There was the Stars collective, which was a group of painters. In film, it was the Fifth Generation. In literature, you have the Scar literature movement, then the Search for Roots Movement, then the avant-garde movement. A literary journal called *Today* arises, and there's a group of writers associated with that. There are the Misty Poets who write these kind of obscure works that, in some ways, are engaging with the recent history, and in some ways, are doing other experimental things.

In short, the cultural scene in China in the '80s is just on fire. The Fifth Generation is a big part of that. They're a group that really redefines cinema, both in terms of content and form, and they were doing very interesting, experimental things, interesting meditations on modern Chinese history and what Chinese culture was. In some ways, they were fuelled by those literary and other cultural movements like the Search for Roots Movement. If you look at early Fifth Generation films like *Yellow Earth* or *Raise the Red Lantern*, you can certainly see the influence of the Search for Roots and the avant-garde movements and what's happening in literature during that time. In fact, most of the major Fifth Generation works were all literary adaptations of contemporary Chinese stories of that era. So there's a lot of interaction and collaboration among the arts during that period.

What's interesting about this revolution is that it happens from within the system, so to speak. Earlier in our conversation we talked about the state-sponsored film studios. These are filmmakers working within those state-sponsored film studios. Some of the films were banned, but in most cases they were being distributed.

The next generation of filmmakers, the Sixth Generation, starts off working as underground, independent filmmakers. That was kind of the birth of independent filmmaking in China.

Now it's not the case, but, at that stage, independent cinema was synonymous with underground, which was synonymous with illegal cinema, because this was made beyond the eyes of the state.

In the early '90s you start getting these Sixth Generation works, with filmmakers like Wang Xiaoshuai and Zhang Yuan. They were making very interesting films. The films are experimental in terms of their structure and subject matter. Often the protagonists of these films are prostitutes, artists, homosexuals—people who are on the margins of society in China. The filmmakers' attention naturally gravitates to these marginalized figures, and they themselves are marginalized figures because of the type of films that they're making.

The next major development in Chinese film was the ascendance of commercial film—which is, right now, really taking over.

**HB**: Is there a bifurcation, as it were, between the Chinese cinema equivalent of Hollywood and the Chinese cinema equivalent of independent small films? Do you see the same sort of structure that you have in the United States? Are we moving towards that sort of a world in Chinese cinema?

**MB**: Yes, I would say so. Mainstream cinema is getting very commercial, very profit-driven, and films like the Sixth Generation films are increasingly harder and harder to make. In one sense, they're easier, technically speaking, because of digital cameras, which are more affordable. And you don't need a whole crew.

When the Sixth Generation were making their films, they were still shooting on film stock. Most of them were borrowing equipment from the Beijing Film Academy on the weekend or on off-hours, but it was still pricey to shoot on film stock. In the digital age, there has been an incredible liberation because now anybody can be a filmmaker.

But at the same time, the space to screen those films is shrinking, because the state is often not condoning a lot of those independent ventures.

**HB**: You talked about it being more profit-driven, more commercial, with the big studios dominating and all that. I understand that economically. But it doesn't necessarily follow that what's "more commercial" in one environment is going to be the same sort of content that's commercial in another environment. One group of people may like to watch Arnold Schwarzenegger blowing things up, but another might like to watch people shelling peas, depending on the proclivities of that environment. Do you get a sense that, not only is the structure becoming more and more like the United States, but that, in fact, the content itself is more or less becoming similar? Or is it not that way?

**MB**: In some ways, the content *is* becoming more similar. There are certain genres that China never had, like the horror movie. If you look at Chinese cinema in mainland China from 1949 to 1978, there weren't really any horror movies. There were some in Hong Kong and Taiwan, but not in mainland China. They also didn't have martial arts movies or romantic comedies.

There are certain genres that are market-driven and market-tested that you see regurgitated over and over in Hollywood that China just never had. But now they're making those kinds of films.

Take Zhang Ziyi. She's one of China's biggest female stars. In 2013 she produced a romantic comedy called *My Lucky Star* and hired an American director named Dennie Gordon—a romantic-comedy director—to go to China and direct it. She basically imported all of the tropes and structures of a romantic comedy into this Chinese film. It did very well in China, but it didn't do very well in America.

I think both Hollywood and Chinese studios are trying to crack the code to find a formula that's going to do equally well in both markets. That's the golden goose that everybody wants to find.

There are some films that are doing very well in the US market that are falling flat in China, or doing well in the Chinese market but are falling flat in the US. There are Hollywood films that do great in China, but so far most of them—I hate to make these blanket statements—are these $100 million blockbusters like *Transformers 4* or *Spiderman 2*. Those films tend to do okay in China.

The problem is that that's a $110 million film to produce, whereas a Chinese film can do the same box office numbers with, say, a $5 million budget. So you can make a film like *My Lucky Star*, a more local production, and do the same box office numbers as *Transformers 4* or something like that. That's an incredible challenge for Hollywood.

**HB**: And presumably, as the economy grows, that imbalance is going to become even greater. As more and more people in China have the purchasing power to buy tickets for movies like *My Lucky Star*, there's going to be even less incentive to go anywhere outside of China to produce those types of films.

**MB**: One thing I've been looking at in my own research recently is this phenomenon of the internalization of Hollywood in the Chinese film market. What I'm seeing is that Chinese audiences still want their Hollywood, they still want their American settings and Hollywood genres and its stars, but they're getting it through local productions.

There were some statistics that came out a few months ago for last year's box office that showed that the Chinese box office had increased overall, but Hollywood profits had dropped. A lot of people were scratching their heads and wondering how that could happen, especially with changes in China's quota system—there is a quota system for foreign films that had just been expanded to allow more foreign films into China.

According to logic, Hollywood's profits should have gone up, so why did they drop? My best guess is that what's happening is local films have been internalizing Hollywood so people are getting their Hollywood experience through local films.

For instance, one of the big box office blockbusters in China recently was a film called *American Dreams in China*, which is about three college friends who start a company to teach English to Chinese students and it becomes a huge success. They have textbooks and videos and they give lectures at stadiums; and then, eventually, these three friends have a falling out and they end up suing each other. The whole story is told in flashback from a law office in New York. A lot of the film was shot on location in New York. The structure is almost identical to *The Social Network*, the 2010 movie about Facebook that came out a few years ago. So the film borrows a lot of the content that's in *The Social Network*, but it's in Chinese, and then it has America as a backdrop, so you have a lot of those elements.

Another one is *My Old Classmate*, which starts off with a very successful New York IT guy who gets an invitation to his old girlfriend's wedding in China, and the film goes back to China and there are flashbacks of their whole relationship. Amongst these are childhood dreams of her going to Stanford and him going to America to study—the whole thing is this grand American Dream.

I could keep listing them. There are many of these films that are engaging with America in a very powerful way, but from a local perspective.

Another way that this is happening is by sometimes featuring Hollywood actors. In 2011, Zhang Yimou made a film called *Flowers of War* (2011) that cast Christian Bale in the lead role. The next year, Feng Xiaogang, one of China's most popular filmmakers, did a film called *Back to 1942*, which starred Adrien Brody and Tim Robbins.

There are a lot of Chinese films that are casting A-level Hollywood talents to try to both appeal to local audiences and brand their films as global products that can be marketed to the world.

## Questions for Discussion:

*1. Will there come a day when American and Chinese audiences effectively have the same taste for "mainstream, commercial films"?*

*2. Do you think that the opportunities provided by digital media to make films more affordably strengthen or diminish cultural diversity?*

# VI. Business and Art

*The Hollywood-Chinese axis vs independent filmmakers*

**HB**: You mentioned your research. My understanding is that you're working on a project right now that looks at the Chinese view of the United States. Is this through cinema, or is this through all sorts of different media from 1949 onwards? How far back does it go?

**MB**: Yes, I'm starting post-1949. In America, we all know about what stereotypes and tropes have been used to portray China in film— think of Charlie Chan and Fu Manchu and all the other racist stereo-types that China has been pigeonholed into. The idea of this project is kind of to reverse the lens and look at the situation from the other perspective: How has China imagined the US during this period?

I look at comic books from the '50s—anti-American comic books after the Korean war—to films and novels. I also look at examples from Taiwan and Hong Kong, so there's a real diversity of perspectives there.

It started off as a project just about portrayals, how America and the figure of the American have been imagined. But increasingly, I'm finding that is intricately intertwined with the structural or industry changes that are taking place—such as these films that I've been mentioning that are shot on location in the US, or are co-productions with Hollywood studios—and the whole way in which the industry is not just portraying America, it's also internalizing aspects of Hollywood.

It's thus becoming more than just a look at texts, but also a look at the way in which cultural industries function, and the interaction between them. Often that interaction is very interesting, and it's only by looking both inside and outside the text that you get the full picture.

For example, there are some films I look at about America which are from the late '70s and early '80s, right after the Reform Era. Basically, these are films that are trying to re-negotiate how you take the old "running dog, imperialist devil" of America and re-embrace them in the age of Sino-US friendship. Those films are trying to dance that dance.

Ultimately the message in these films is, *Sure, America is wonderful and there are a lot of great things that are there, but patriotism trumps all of those temptations.* The protagonists in these films are often given an opportunity to immigrate or marry someone in America, or the long-lost father comes back to take the child back to China to let them inherit his industry. In the end, they all say, *"No, I must stay home and contribute to the building of the motherland,"*—that kind of thing.

There are three or four films like that, that were made in the late '70s and early '80s—one called *Loyal Overseas Chinese Family* (1979), one called *The Herdsman* (1982) one called *Romance On Lushan Mountain* (1980)—and, in fact, the actors who played the protagonists in all three of those films immigrated to the United States a few years after they were made. That gives you a sense of what these films were up against and what they were trying to do—they were explicitly made to convince people *not* to do that. It really shows you how high those stakes were.

**HB**: Are people in China aware of those ironies? Are they aware that the actors who played the protagonists of those films actually left China, or is that something that's not part of the public consciousness?

**MB**: They know, but they left a few years after those films were successful, so they had already probably faded from memory a little bit. It wasn't like the films were released and the next week they emigrated.

**HB**: But sometimes people will look back at an administration or a certain era and they'll say, "*These guys were trying to say that, but look what ended up happening—the very opposite.*" Is that something that is clear in the public consciousness, or not so much?

**MB**: Not so much. I've never seen anybody else write about this phenomenon. There was an immigration wave in the '80s. A lot of Chinese who had either intellectual prospects as graduate students, getting jobs or research fellowships, or people in the arts who could get special visas to go to the US—there were a lot of them going abroad in the '80s, so there was this large immigration wave, and those actors were just one aspect of that. Especially when you get to 1989 and post-1989, there's quite a bit of that going on.

Of course, things come full circle. Present day, all three of those individuals are very active now in the Chinese entertainment industry, directing, producing, or acting in films.

One of them is Joan Chen from *The Last Emperor* (1987). She did very well in Hollywood (she was also in *Twin Peaks* (1992)), but she started out as a film actress in China. She was the star of this film called *Loyal Overseas Chinese Family*, which was one of those typical films about having the opportunity to go abroad, but in the end staying to contribute to the nation. But she left—as did some of those other actors.

**HB**: Is there anything about the Chinese portrayal of American society that really surprised you?

**MB**: Well, what's happening right now is quite surprising. There are new films coming out now like *My Old Classmate* that I've just talked about, and another recently released film called *But Always*—another China-US romance about two lovers who start out in China, one of them immigrates to New York, and they go back and forth between New York and China. There's another one called *American Dreams in China* I also mentioned earlier. There are many movies like this.

The exciting and surprising thing for me is just how deeply ingrained this trend is getting and how much the industries in

Hollywood and China are becoming tied to one another. As this project is unfolding, it's almost like I can't even keep up with the changes that are happening. DreamWorks Animation Studios just opened up Oriental DreamWorks in Shanghai. Relativity Media just did a major deal with a Chinese collaborator. One after another, major Hollywood studios are getting involved in deals with Chinese studios.

**HB**: So it's the speed at which it's happening that's shocking?

**MB**: The speed and the pervasiveness. Just look at the market for American franchise action movies over the last few years. Virtually every, major franchise—*The Expendables, Resident Evil, X-Men, Iron Man*, and there are many others—has started casting major Chinese actors in those films.

This was unthinkable just a couple years ago, but right now China is the number two film market in the world, and it's set to become number one in a couple of years—these American studios want a piece of that market. In some cases, that means a co-production. In other cases it means better access to the Chinese market by casting known Chinese talent so that your film will play better to those audiences. That's really changing the way films are being made, and it's perhaps changing Hollywood just as much as it's changing China.

**HB**: I can imagine that one possible formula would be to have a romantic comedy film where one protagonist is Chinese and the other is an American, rather than having the Chinese couple that is tempted to go to America, or the "American in China" experience. That seems like the kind of film that would naturally appeal to both sides. Are we going to see more films like that, do you think?

**MB**: There have been some, and there probably will be more. They're going to keep trying to "crack the code", so to speak, but maybe there is no "code" to crack. Maybe you just have to make a good film.

Because, honestly, if I look at a lot of these films—well, they aren't very good. For me, as a film scholar, they are interesting as phenomenon, in terms of what they're saying about America and what they're saying about this relationship between the United States and China. But are they masterpieces that are going to stand the test of time?

**HB**: I'm guessing not.

**MB**: That's a pretty safe bet, I think. If you were to ask me what's the most exciting thing happening, aesthetically, in terms of who's really breaking ground in the Chinese film industry right now, who can challenge you intellectually and push you into places that are going to make you think and be unsettled, I would point you to those independent films that are getting shut down at the Beijing Independent Film Festival.

There are some truly incredible people working in the independent film industry, especially documentary film people like Du Haibin and Hu Jie. They are making incredibly powerful films. But that stuff is getting shut down.

**HB**: That's pretty alarming, isn't it? Perhaps even more alarming than the spectre of independent filmmakers here being squeezed out for economic factors. There, you have the same sorts of factors—namely economic—but you also have the hand of the state involved in shutting them down.

The obvious question is, what might we be able to do about that, or how might we be able to move towards a happier future where those voices are heard and, at the very least, not eliminated?

**MB**: Right now those voices are basically subsisting on a couple of small festivals in China that are sometimes cancelled and sometimes not, or film clubs and universities that will sometimes screen these films. They are very much reliant on the international film festival circuit, or universities—every year I bring a couple of these filmmakers to our campus.

But it's really tough for them. There are also a couple of TV stations, like Phoenix TV in Hong Kong, which will often broadcast these documentaries, so the filmmakers will get certain royalties through those broadcast rights. But right now there's not a lot of space for them to exist in China, or at least practice their art in an open way and have their films distributed. It really is David vs. Goliath.

I mentioned Hu Jie a moment ago as one of these figures. He has a film called *Though I Am Gone* about the Cultural Revolution. It's a first-person perspective documentary about a man talking about the Cultural Revolution and his wife, who died during that period.

It just tears you down when you watch this film. There's a scene where he has this chest in which he saves all these relics of his former wife, and he opens it up and shows all these watches and articles of clothing; he shows you her soiled underpants from when she was beaten and killed. It's such powerful work, and no one in China can see it.

And probably as equally powerful as the content of the film is that, at the very end, there's a line that says, *Please distribute this—* that is to say, please make it available and put it online for free: just get it out there. Now you can go to YouTube and find this film.

For me, this is kind of the way out, a way forward. On the one hand, you've got the capitalist monster and all these Hollywood-inspired commercial blockbusters, but here's somebody who—not just aesthetically in terms of content of the film, but even in terms of the distribution—is just going totally around all of that and making a powerful statement.

## Questions for Discussion:

*1. Do you think that there will be any effective difference between Hollywood and the Chinese film industry in 30 years?*

*2. Have you watched **Though I am Gone** on YouTube?*

# VII. Flourishing
*The power of values*


**HB**: I'd like to return to the question of censorship, both in cinema and literature.

My sense is that the possibility of exerting any international pressure to alleviate this sort of censorship is becoming less and less of an option as more and more governments and private companies are electing to sidestep the issues due to "economic realities", or "opportunities", or however we should call it (perhaps simply "greed").

It's not entirely clear to me that it would have been possible to change things that way anyway, but I'm guessing that there's even less motivation on the part of third parties to do so than there ever was, and that will likely diminish even further as time goes on.

The question then becomes one of how to concretely move forwards. What do you think can be, or should be, done? Let me put it more concretely: if you were President of the United States, how would you engage with China on the cultural front, and what sorts of measures would you take?

**MB**: I'm not a politician.

**HB**: I know. That's why I'm asking you.

**MB**: Well, there's a reason I didn't go that route: so I wouldn't have to answer these kinds of questions and deal with those thorny problems.

But I will say this: like we said earlier, in order to have both a healthy cultural environment and healthy market, you need these different voices. I think, at the core, the Chinese government needs to have more confidence in itself. It should be able to embrace criticism and different voices. It's not going to fall apart.

The reality is that many of these independent films are very critical, but these are, after all, experimental documentary films that are not going to reach a huge audience anyway. Realistically, how many of the younger generation are going to watch these things?

It's already a marginalized art form. You don't need to squash it out like that. I don't know if they look at them as cockroaches. Maybe they do. But you can let some of them crawl around. They're not going to hurt anybody. But once you start trying to stamp them out, it says something about your own belief in yourself. I think China's government needs to have more confidence to embrace these different voices, and I think they'll find that doing so is not the end of the world, by any means.

In some ways it will actually help reinvigorate other aspects of the cultural industry. In film, for example, a lot of these very creative voices, after cutting their teeth and making experimental films or documentaries, will likely filter into the commercial film network. If you look at the Sixth Generation filmmakers, they started off as uncompromisingly experimental, doing really radical things in terms of film, but most of them now are so-called "above ground" filmmakers, making films about very safe topics that are widely distributed. The Fifth Generation filmmakers also had some films that were banned, but now they're also very safe. It's a familiar story: you get older, more conservative, and you're not rebelling all the time.

Look at Lou Ye. He's a fiction filmmaker who's made several incredible films, many of them on explosive topics. For example, he made a film called *Summer Palace* (2006), which depicts the events leading up to the 1989 massacre. He's somebody who's gotten into trouble over the years with the state. But he is an incredible filmmaker, somebody with such a powerful voice and identity and vision. If you watch a few frames of one of his films, you can say, "*That's a Lou Ye film.*"

I would love to see China be more confident in terms of what they feel they can allow. A lot of China's policies concerning the policing of the arts go back to the 1942 Yan'an Talks on Art and Literature that Mao Zedong gave, where he basically said that there's "correct art" and "incorrect art".

He said that correct art should serve the workers, peasants, and soldiers. It should be talking to the broad masses so that it's understandable and not opaque. It should have clear-cut heroes and villains—all that kind of stuff. It was basically the prescription for how art should be produced; and that drove all artistic production for the next four decades in China.

That kind of a policy is largely dead and gone now, but the ghost still haunts the state. I think a lot of the cultural bureaucrats in China still look at art as "correct" or "incorrect" and I feel that we need to move past that age. There is no correct or incorrect art. But I do think that is one of the many ghosts haunting contemporary China that has carried over from the socialist era.

**HB**: I have two more questions. The first one is, do you still talk to Mr Jensen?

**MB**: I do. Every couple of months I give him a call, and over the years, he's written me a couple of letters and I've saved every one of them. Some of them are the most beautiful things anybody has ever written to me.

Several years ago he recommended me for induction into my high school's alumni hall of fame. I couldn't go because I was teaching, but he gave the induction speech and he sent me his handwritten speech in an old Coca-Cola bottle. It's several pages long. But he put it in a bottle, because he said, "*As a teacher, you feel like you're stranded on a desert island. You're always there, but the students come and go. You feel like you're always sending them these messages in a bottle, but you never know if they got the message.*"

And he added, "*On very rare occasions, not only does somebody get the message, but they understand it so fully and completely that they grasp it even better than you did.*"

After I graduated high school, he was diagnosed with cancer and they thought it was terminal. They gave him two or three years. But, together with his wonderful wife, they completely revamped their diet and did all kinds of research and they fought this thing until the end; and he beat it. He has been cancer-free for many years.

But during those dark days when he was very ill, several of his former students got together, and one of them wrote to Kurt Vonnegut—because he used to teach us *Slaughterhouse Five*, as I mentioned earlier—and told him about our teacher. And Kurt Vonnegut wrote Mr Jensen a letter. Another one of them wrote to Robert Pirsig, the author of *Zen and the Art of Motorcycle Maintenance*, and he also sent Mr Jensen a little postcard.

What that told me was that he wasn't on such a solitary island after all, because he clearly affected a lot of people other than me. Just the fact that former students would do that shows what an impact he had on a lot of people.

A few months ago, he sent me the Robert Pirsig postcard. He passed it on saying it would be better off in my hands. That's a relationship that I really treasure. I wouldn't be sitting here, nor would I have even done half the things I've done in my life, if it weren't for him.

**HB**: I'm sure that, as a teacher and educator yourself, you're well aware of the power that you have, in terms of framing ideas and opening up worlds to your students. It must be quite inspiring.

**MB**: It is. I'll even tell the Mr Jensen story in class sometimes. I generally like to keep my classes to content, but when I teach 4th year Chinese—a language class—as long as I'm speaking Chinese, anything goes. So sometimes I'll tell them the Mr Jensen story in Chinese, and assign a student to interpret it to work on her interpretation skills.

One year when I did that, there was a girl in the class who, when she graduated, gave me a card saying, "*You might not remember it, but you told us this story about your high school teacher and that changed my life.*"

So I've been able to pass on this experience in that way. I hope that his story will continue to resonate with more people. I certainly try to get it out there. He gave me a gift, and I feel that the best way to reciprocate is for me to pass that on and keep giving that gift.

**HB**: Well, we'll certainly do what we can to pass the story along. One last question: Do you think that your knowledge of Chinese has made you a somewhat different person than you might otherwise have been?

**MB**: Without question. Like we talked about earlier, a language isn't just a hardware, it's a different way of looking at the world. It makes you step out of your comfort zone and out of your own shoes in terms of, not just the way you see things, but even your values. Every culture and every language has its own set of perspectives, values, sense of what's important, and its own way of telling stories.

For example, I've done a lot of translation as you know, and there have been many opportunities over the years where I had to take something I wrote in English and then write it in Chinese for a differ-ent publication venue, or vice versa. Every time I'm in one of those situations, I never translate my own work. I rewrite it, because the way I would convey that message in English is very different than how I would say it in Chinese, or vice versa.

It's not just an issue of language, it's a different perspective. Of course, if you had to summarize each article, the summary in each language might be very similar, if not almost identical, but the way it's conveyed, that way of storytelling, is very different.

When I stepped into that other cultural world at 19, that set me on a path and gave me this alternative perspective and an alternative perspective on myself as well. People talk about "culture shock"—I didn't feel a lot of culture shock when I went to China, simply because I went with my arms open and just wanted to have all kinds of new experiences. But when I came *back*, that was an *incredible* culture shock, because I had changed so radically, but when I came back I found that nothing had changed here.

Interacting with the people I grew up with—that was very diffi-cult when I first came back after that intense year or two in China. For me, that was the biggest culture shock. And that shock is directly a response to the question you just asked: it's because I had transformed in such a fundamental way and had seen things and been exposed to things that I had never been exposed to before. That changes you; and there's no going back.

As an educator, I think the best thing that our students can do is get out of that comfort zone, open up more of these doors, study abroad and learn different languages, be exposed to these other perspectives.

It's not easy. Learning languages isn't easy. It's a lot of hard work. And living in foreign cultures where you're not comfortable and the rules of the game are all different also isn't easy.

**HB**: But it's not about being easy.

**MB**: Right, exactly. That's the point. Everyone knows the famous phrase from the Declaration of Independence: *Life, Liberty, and the Pursuit of Happiness*. I think the pursuit of happiness—having fun, things being easy—that dominates the lives of our students.

But what's meaningful often isn't equated with fun, or happiness, or those fluffy kind of sentiments. Often, if you want to live a life that brings your actions in congruence with your values, it's very hard work, but the payoffs are boundless.

So, yes, I've been changed forever by that experience. And I wouldn't have it any other way.

**HB**: Is there anything else you'd like to add? Anything that we've missed?

**MB**: No.

**HB**: Well, thank you very much Michael. I really enjoyed this.

**MB**: Me too. My pleasure.

# Questions for Discussion:

*1. Do you agree that too many people are preoccupied with "having fun" and taking "easy pathways"? If so, how might that best be corrected?*

*2. Do you think that Michael would have ended up doing something similar to what he is doing now if he hadn't gone on a study-abroad program to China in his sophomore year?*

## Continuing the Conversation

Readers interested in a more detailed treatment of some of the topics discussed in this conversation are referred to Michael's book of interviews with Chinese filmmakers, *Speaking in Images,* his book, *A History of Pain: Trauma in Modern Chinese Literature and Film*, together with his many English translations of contemporary Chinese literature, including *Wuhan Diary*, *To Live*, *Remains of Life*, *Wild Kids* and *The Song of Everlasting Sorrow*.

# Babbling Barbarians

## How Translators Keep Us Civilized

### A conversation with David Bellos

# Introduction

*Teaching a Man to Fish*

One of the few advantages to discovering that one has careened precipitously into middle age is that there is less and less motivation to keep up appearances. A related consequence of this vastly more relaxed attitude towards my own ignorance is that few things now cause me greater pleasure than being confronted with solid evidence that I have unthinkingly adopted a wildly inappropriate stereotype.

So it is that David Bellos, writer, translator and Director of Princeton University's Program in Translation and Intercultural Communication, has given me a good deal of satisfaction.

Because I must admit that, until recently, I never thought that translation was a particularly interesting topic. But when I picked up his book, *Is That A Fish in Your Ear? Translation and the Meaning of Everything*, I discovered it to be a delightful potpourri of seemingly casual reflections that methodically explode great chunks of the "conventional wisdom" about translation and language that we have unthinkingly saddled ourselves with.

How many of us have mindlessly parroted the line: *"A translation is no substitute for the original"*, despite the fact that even a moment's studied reflection will make it painfully apparent that nothing could be further from the truth: a substitute for the original is, of course, exactly what any translation is.

Examine, too, the unsuspectingly subtle notion of a 'native language'. There's precious little ambiguity when referring to a thirty-year-old Englishman who is struggling to make himself understood at the *boulangerie* during a quick jaunt across the Channel, but what of the

Polish immigrant who moved to Sydney at the age of 7? By the time she enters university, is Polish still her "mother tongue" despite the fact that she vastly prefers to express herself in English?

The closer one looks at these "obvious" definitions and categorizations, the less obvious they start to appear.

And then there is the act of translation itself.

Throughout the ages, much ink has been spilled on how inferior "literal" or "word-for-word" translations are from a more "holistic" approach, which is a curious state of affairs given that virtually no professional translator or commentator has ever suggested that approach in the first place.

A natural starting point to examine the whole issue of "literal translation" is St. Jerome's groundbreaking 4th-century efforts to convert the Bible into Latin. In a letter to his friend Pammachius describing his translation philosophy, St. Jerome admits to liberally converting the overall gist of the passage, except when concerning himself with translating the sacred scriptures from Greek, where *"even the order of the words is a* **mysterium***."*

So that's pretty straightforward: St. Jerome's translation methodology is to focus on conveying the essential meaning of the text in every case except that where he happens to be occupying himself with Greek texts of the sacred scriptures.

But David points out the confusion rapidly reasserts itself after a minute or two of more serious consideration:

> *"That seems clear until you realize that the exception clause drives a cart and horses through the main claim, because what Jerome did throughout his long life was to translate sacred scripture, more than half of which he translated from Greek."*

Moreover, and even more confusingly, it turns out that the true meaning of St. Jerome's highlighted *mysterium* at the heart of his explanation is, ironically enough, unknown.

*"At the root of Western arguments about how best to translate lies a mystery-word that nobody is quite sure how to translate."*

Well, OK. Words are notoriously complicated, messy things. But one thing that we surely cannot question is that the job of a translator is to safely transport the meaning of the original words into the promised land of another language.

Except that, on closer inspection, meaning turns out to be a particularly slippery thing; a frustratingly transient amalgam of intonations, past experiences and contexts that hang side by side with standard dictionary definitions.

In the film *The Great Escape*, for example, there is a famous scene where an English-speaking character is exposed by a German guard after he unthinkingly responds to an otherwise benign English phrase that the guard spontaneously puts to him. Bellos chooses this example because it is an extreme case where context is not only vital, it is effectively all there is: the true meaning of the incident is actually completely independent of the words exchanged. The guard actually said *"Good luck"* and the escapee reflexively replied *"Thank you"*, but the exchange could just as easily have been: *"Your fly is open"*; *"No it's not"* or *"What time is it?"*; *"Ten to eight".*

*"Written and spoken language don't have a meaning just like that, on their own, in themselves. In fact, the only way of being sure whether an utterance has any meaning at all is to get someone to translate it for you."*

So far, so amusing. But behind all this playfulness lies a serious point.

When we speak or write, David maintains, we are most certainly communicating information. But we are doing much more than that as well. After all, if that was all that was going on, there'd be no need for us to all sound different from each other or each have a unique literary style. But we do.

At the beginning of our Princeton conversation, I asked David if there was some subject he was particularly motivated to touch on, some point he was most excited to convey.

*"Ask me why we don't all speak the same language",* he urged me. So I did.

*"The answer to that,"* he gushed excitedly, *"is that we don't want to."* Then he laughed and blurted out, as if to clearly contrast this point from the many other provocative speculations he'd indulged in for the last hour or so, *"And I'm quite sure of this."*

From different accents, to different pitches, to different turns of phrases to entirely different languages, every act of speech is a form of individuation, of declaiming our separate uniqueness.

We could all sound the same if we really wanted to, David declared. We could all be like Meryl Streep and imitate one another. It's not a question of acting ability; it's a question of will.

> *"Individual diction and forms of speech do not vary because they need to for any physical, intellectual or practical reasons. Individual speech varies because one of the fundamental, perhaps original, purposes of speaking is to serve as a differentiating tool—to say 'I am not you but me.'"*

This, for David, is a key point, the central thrust of his argument. A touch of focused seriousness suddenly entered our conversation as he began to speak more excitedly.

> *"If the only way we think about language is as a means of communication, then all these different ways of speaking would be completely useless and pointless. And language would be a totally different kind of thing.*

> *"It is in the nature of language to be different. Meanwhile, the push towards making language the same—standard languages, written languages—is another dimension of our social organization and cultural lives, and these two dimensions are in permanent tension.*

*Translation is in the middle between these two things: it represents these two tensions of being completely unique and of being sharable.*"

"*And that,*" he concludes, slowing down once more, a gentle smile returning to his lips, *"is why it's so interesting."*

Which it now so obviously seems to be.

# The Conversation

# I. Introductory Musings

*On Perec, Chomsky, and other matters*

**HB**: I'd like to talk a minute about what it means to speak a language well—speaking a "good Russian," or a "good English" or a "good French"—which naturally transcends knowing the generally appropriate words for things. You must have met many people who speak particularly well, who use language particularly incisively. Isn't that what we mean by speaking a good Russian, or a good French?

**DB**: It ought to be. One ought to allow oneself to react to creative, striking, appropriate, colourful use of language—whatever its variety, whatever its particular form of diction or accent. Yet there is a long history of otherwise sophisticated people casting others into the outer darkness of foolishness and idiocy because their form of speech is different, or is perceived as comical. There is something bizarre in hearing other forms of speech as either nonsense or comical when they don't correspond to our dialect or what we recognize as a prestigious dialect.

**HB**: Like the patronizing "bar-bar-bar" reaction of the ancient Greeks when faced with someone speaking a foreign tongue. *"You're a funny person who speaks differently, so you're a barbarian..."*

**DB**: Yes. I would like to hope that most speakers of English now are not as outrageously linguistically nationalistic as the ancient Greeks. But somehow the form of language is about making distinctions, and where it's social distinctiveness that matters and social hierarchy that matters, then language becomes a vector of not terribly nice forms of social rivalry.

**HB**: You mention these sentiments quite explicitly in the epilogue of your book, *Is That A Fish in Your Ear? Translation and the Meaning of Everything*, and I hope to have the chance to explore them in more detail later on.

But let me first back up and ask you about your own personal experience of becoming a translator, which seemed to strongly overlap with your first encounter with the French writer Georges Perec. I think many people would naturally have the question, *"How does one become a translator, anyway? How does that whole process start?"* How did it begin for you?

**DB**: In 1981, I was teaching at the University of Edinburgh. A colleague met me in the corridor and shoved a book in my hand saying: *"I couldn't finish this, but I know you're going to like it".* It was *Life: A User's Manual*—a French paperback copy. I hadn't read Perec. I vaguely knew the name, but I'd never read him. I took it home and started reading it and was entranced.

Very fortunately, I then caught a bad cold and I had to take three days off work and stay in bed, which gave me a chance to read it right the way through. I don't know if this has happened to you, but it's rare in modern life that you really do get the opportunity to read a long book right the way through from beginning to end.

**HB**: And it is a long book.

**DB**: It is a long book. But having a stuffy head and streamy eyes and everybody feeling sorry for me and bringing me cups of tea was a perfect environment in which to be completely ensconced inside the world of Perec.

And as I enthusiastically read through, there glimmered even then in that first reading the thought that, *This is a book in French, but it's a book that belongs to the world. I would love to be able to share this with other people.* I was convinced that it was going to work in English.

Modern French fiction, from the late 50s to the early 80s, had been a very special field called "the new novel"—without characters, without psychology—that had acquired a little prestige, but in a sense it almost killed the pleasures of reading.

So by the time I finished that first reading of *La Vie Mode d'Emploi*, the idea had occurred to me that it would be really great, if only to do something different with my life, to translate this book into English. At that time I was a teacher of French, I was a specialist in 19th-century fiction and wasn't a 20th-century person at all. But, I thought, maybe this could be done. It took a while, and it was quite an adventure with many ups and downs. But within a few years an American publisher had signed me up for it, and I was able to take six months off my job just to translate *La Vie Mode d'Emploi.*

So you could say I became a translator for Perec or you could say thank goodness I met Perec, because encountering Perec is what taught me how to translate.

**HB**: Do you think he influenced your style at all? It seems to me that there is a stylistic similarity between both of you, particularly when it comes to playing with language. For example, in *Is That A Fish in Your Ear?*, you seem to take great pleasure in inverting phrases. You may not even be aware of it yourself, but for me it was quite striking. You say: *"dictionaries are not necessary for translation, translations are necessary for dictionaries"* or *"the ineffable is not the enemy of translation, translation is the enemy of the ineffable".*

**DB**: I hope I haven't done it too often...

**HB**: No. But it does give the book a certain sense of playfulness that I thought might be shared with the likes of Georges Perec.

**DB**: I think my initial enthusiasm for Perec does have something to do with a stylistic affinity, but not so much on the level of playfulness, because *Life: A User's Manual*, despite its complexity and the fact that it has some quite extraordinary games in particular places, actually has a fairly plain narrative style. It's not elaborate, fancy rhetorically-sophisticated French. It's very British and understated; and that's one of the reasons that I thought this would work well in English.

I thought to myself: *I don't have to do a great deal of work to most of this text to make it say what it says in an English that I can write.* That's to say: fairly plain, fairly precise and not very rhetorical English.

That, I think, is a point of affinity, a point of meeting between my style and *Life: A User's Manual*, which I guess is why I thought I could do it. The playfulness—the making of puns and the juggling with language—that I learned later, but also from Perec. Perec's other books that I went on to read and learn and love have a lot of fun with the potential of language—to bend it and make it say other things.

So, yes, Perec taught me to write. My father also told me about puns—he was a great punner. But I don't know—it's probably easier for other people to make these judgments. It's very hard for me because, of course, having translated Perec, what Perec says is what I wrote, and it's difficult to separate myself from that, even after all this time. It was a long time ago that I began that adventure.

**HB**: One of the things that I think is very engaging for somebody who will pick up *Is That A Fish In Your Ear?* is this sense of being confronted with clichés that most of us have taken on faith and accepted and sometimes even unthinkingly regurgitated in turn. You examine them and often explode them.

The one that certainly caught my eye at the very beginning was this common notion that "a translation is not a substitute for the original." That's a phrase that most of us have heard, and doubtless many of us may even have said, but you point out very cogently that this is just absurd: a translation *is* a substitute for the original—in fact that's exactly what translation is.

Why is it, do you think, that we've adopted such evidently incorrect clichés when it comes to something like translation? Why do people believe that translation is no substitute for the original when, in fact, that's of course exactly what it is, and any reasonable person will realize that upon a moment's reflection?

**DB**: May I give you a long answer?

**HB**: I gave you a long question, so go right ahead and give me a long answer.

**DB**: A number of years ago I went to a Class Day, which is the day of the year when students graduate, and their parents come and we have a big reception. It's just about the only time of the year when we meet their parents, and it's generally all very pleasant.

I was chatting with a group of parents and mentioned that I run the program in translation at Princeton. Then one particularly plump and pink parent replied, in a most challenging way, *"Ah, yes but a translation is never a substitute for the original, is it?"*.

Of course, I'm on my best behaviour right then and couldn't say, *"Oh, shut up you silly old..."* But somehow I was just so irritated by hearing it in that environment, and as a put-down as well, that I got on my bicycle, pedalled home and starting writing a diatribe. And it suddenly came to me as to why this was such a silly thing to say. That's actually where my book, *Is That A Fish in Your Ear?*, began: that first little squib.

And having written my little squib—dashing it off in an afternoon—I was rather pleased with it. And I thought, *Well, there are some other things like that get up my nose, so maybe I should get them off my chest too.*

So over the following couple of weeks I wrote three or four more little ten-page things and showed them to my son who is a real writer—he's a journalist and a writer of non-fiction books. He looked at it and said, *"You know, dad, if you go on like this, you might earn a real living,"* or words to that effect.

I took it as very encouraging to get even indirect interest from Alex, but I did nothing for the short-term. Still, the idea that there could be a general interest book about translation that was not technical, not boring and not ponderous, grew in my mind. Then, six or eight months later, just walking around this corner right outside my house at the beginning of a term of study leave in which I was going to travel and do all sorts of things, I slipped on the ice and broke my ankle. So I was confined to barracks for several weeks.

**HB**: It's just like that cold that you had when first reading Perec.

**DB**: Yes, that's right.

**HB**: Bed is your best friend.

**DB**: Yes: self-harm is an amazingly productive circumstance for me. So anyway, I was stuck in my study. I had my leg in plaster and I had to use crutches. So I went back to the scribblings I'd done the previous year and I thought, *Well, maybe I should expand that a bit.* And so it just grew, really, like that. It was based, of course, on a lot of teaching I've done and a lot of talks I'd been to, and the wonderful resources of the library here, which I can get online. I wasn't writing it for any particular series or for any particular purpose. It was the first thing I've written, actually, without any sort of finality in mind.

When it was about half done, I had the cheek to show it to a literary agent, asking, *"Do you think this could be of interest to anybody?"* I was extremely lucky because she took a liking to it and gave me some very good advice about how to reshape it and turn it into a fuller thing. And that's how that book came to be. It was written really quite fast in the end—except, of course, that I've really been writing it for 40 years.

The question of translation and substitution, and the original and the authentic, is an issue that I've been battling with for my whole career as a teacher of foreign languages and literatures in the English-speaking world. We have departments of French, and departments of Italian, and departments of Russian, and then we have this funny thing called 'comparative literature,' which is held at arms length by colleagues within the language disciplines, who say, *"But they do it in translation; and, of course, translation is no substitute for the original—you can't actually do Balzac or Cervantes or anything else properly unless you read them in the original."*

I am not a very political person. I used to just negotiate my way through this without ever really clarifying to myself why this was a silly argument. Actually it wasn't really about originals and translations at all: it was about ranking, it was about hierarchy, it was about turf.

And it was—most paradoxically and peculiarly, given that the proponents of the idea that "translation is no substitute for the original" are mostly people who *can* read it in the original—a way of keeping the foreign at bay, or keeping it very closed.

And this, not necessarily inadvertently, gives lots of monoglot English speakers a jolly good reason—a cover story, as it were—for not being interested in anything beyond these shores.

That's the conclusion I came to, and that's what powered the writing of this book: that, actually, things people say about translation always mean something else, or they have an application that is not to do with translation but with all sorts of different things: mostly social, relational, ideological things. I don't like using that word 'ideology' too much, but this really is an ideological issue.

**HB**: I have two follow-up questions. My first one is not terribly substantive but driven by my curiosity: the person who originally harassed you and provoked you at that Class Day—the pink and plump parent—have you given him or her a copy of your book?

**DB**: No, I don't remember who it was and it really doesn't matter. If he knows who he is, all I will say is, I'm very grateful. I feel grateful to be needled in that way because, while he said it to me on that particular day, millions of people have said it to millions of other people. He's not responsible for this. So, thank you very much for setting me off on this track which has been great fun since then.

**HB**: One of the goals of your book seemed to be to connect with some fraction of English speakers who might not appreciate, given the fact that English is the most dominant language in the world today, the subtleties of translation, or the necessity of translation, or the import and impact of translation, as much as somebody who would speak another language.

Have you had any feedback from people who've read your book and thus felt motivated to now read other works in translation? Have people told you, *"I read your book and now I realize these clichés are perhaps a silly way to look at things, and I've now begun reading all these other works in translation."* Have you had much of that?

**DB**: Well, I've had a very copious mailbag, both material and electronic, from all over the world, actually. My favourite reader's letter is from a girl in Azerbaijan. How she got hold of the book I don't know—presumably on a download from Kindle or something. And it's inspired her, or so she tells me in her email, to want to become a translator. That's great.

Obviously most of the people who write to an author about a book do so because they've got something to say, and it's usually something like, *"Are you sure about this?"* I've had a lot of corrections. The paperback edition has quite a number of corrections from the first hardback edition. And for all those readers who've written in to tell me that I got this or that little bit wrong here or there, I'm very grateful. That's what a book is like: it's a conversation with readers. And since I touch on an absurdly wide range of topics—most of which I am not at all expert in—it's not surprising that there are little tweaks and twiddles to get it properly right.

I've not had any really negative letters or negative feedback. That's what slightly worries me, because it seems to me that I do stick my neck out rather a long way and I do pursue some rather grand and general arguments, and it cannot possibly be the case that I am so indisputably right about everything that it wouldn't be possible to write a serious critique of my position. But I haven't seen that yet.

**HB**: Well, it's early days yet. Take heart.

**DB**: Yes, that's right.

**HB**: Changing gears a bit: one of the things in your book that I found very amusing and interesting were some comments that you made about various Chomskyan ideas—in particular there was this distinction between sentences that were grammatically correct and sentences that actually had meaning.

You mention a particular phrase, "colourless green ideas sleep furiously," that Chomsky has used in one of his early works to demonstrate that, while grammatically correct, it clearly couldn't convey any meaningful content.

Then within a very short time, weeks perhaps, there were some clever students at Stanford who developed all sorts of perfectly meaningful contexts in which "colourless green ideas sleep furiously" actually is completely coherent, and perhaps even a beautiful or fitting metaphor for various different ideas.

On the one hand this is clearly very amusing. But on the other hand, it strikes me, a layperson, as more than just idle game-playing and perhaps indicative of something deeper. Aren't these clever re-interpretations by the Stanford students illustrating that there is no *a priori* line between language and meaning? Doesn't this demonstrate that it is not the case that you can separate language so cleanly into the respective categories of grammar and meaning?

**DB**: You put me in a delightfully unique position in my life to take the defense of Chomsky, which is not something I often do.

But to take the defense of Chomsky, *Syntactic Structures* is a truly revolutionary work about language, and to put it in a very simple nutshell what it says is that the science of language is about grammar, not about meaning. It is about mind and thought and the processes that have to be supposed to go on for grammar to exist.

And through the entire adventure of universal grammar, there is no important distinction made between what is language and what a language is.

For me that's an important thing, but from the Chomskyan side of things—which is perfectly coherent and perfectly straightforward— the distinction between those two makes no difference. It doesn't want to bother with meaning, because meaning is about the world and all sorts of things that aren't linguistics.

Linguistics is a study or an attempt to approach the core issue of the underlying structure of verbal expression, and that's called grammar. So the point of Chomsky's example is to say: *"You have to leave meaning out, because grammar doesn't deal with meaning."* Because you can have grammatical sentences that mean nothing at all. That's the point of his example of colourless green ideas sleeping furiously. It comes right at the beginning and it's to clear away the semantic complications: it's not what words *mean*, it's how the grammar works.

The fact that people can play with a generally nonsensical sentence and find a context in which it is not nonsensical is of no consequence to Chomsky. People do all sorts of things with language all the time that aren't part of what his linguistics is about.

I'm not a Chomskyan, I don't do that sort of thing. I am interested in what people do with language and with the way in which language is actually part of human behaviour. It's integrated into all sorts of things that have nothing to do with grammar but to do with interpersonal relations, to do with expression, to do with commanding and obeying and promising. And that's not Chomsky's field at all.

**HB**: OK, but I think I still might be missing something. Surely what we're doing right now—well, hopefully what we're doing right now, at any rate—is imparting and exchanging meaning with each other. When one talks about looking at language and doing it in a meaning-independent way, I'm no longer sure what we're talking about (as it were).

Sure, we can probe certain issues related to what extent we can define meaning and how universal things are and so forth and so on. But the very idea that we're going to study communication, we're going to study language, and yet we'll say, *"Well, I don't care about meaning at all"*, strikes me as very odd indeed. It's like saying, *"We're going to study physics, but we don't care about the natural world."*

I mean, I just don't understand what we're talking about at that point: are we just talking about sound waves that are being uttered back and forth, or some formal structure of the human brain? I find myself pretty confused by all of this.

**DB**: Well, it is a confusion and a great division in the world of the study of language. I'm not competent enough to give you a more eloquent or more detailed exposition of the Chomskyan pursuit of universal grammar, which continues. I can't really judge how far they have gotten.

But one point where their approach and my kind of more socially, culturally-oriented studies of language do actually converge, is the doubt as to whether we are talking about the same thing when it comes to communication and language. Communication is possible in all sorts of channels and media.

If the study of language is the study of communication, then on the one hand that dissolves language into a much vaster field of inquiry.

On the other hand, it quite possibly misrepresents language. Or rather it's like—as Chomsky said himself once during a talk—that it would be like trying to do the physics of the human eye by using material only from watching television. Sure we use the eye to watch television, and we use language to communicate meanings, but are you sure that's all we do when we are engaged in active language? I'm not so sure that all I am doing with you is imparting a little thought from my brain into yours.

Speech—and writing too, but speech most obviously—has all sorts of functions that are not easily captured by this word 'communication', if you think of communication as the transmission of some distinct chunk of information that is sent from here to there.

**HB**: So, what else does language do besides communication?

**DB**: Well, there's a huge difference between you saying what you've just said in that tone of voice with that pitch and with that intonation and you saying it in some other pitch.

If you were to stand up and shout what you just said, it would not be the same human interaction. The linguistic meaning would be exactly the same—or at least the meaning that you could deduce from it being written down, that is—that would be the same.

All sorts of things are going on: relational things, turn-taking, gesticulation, modulation of voice. These are part of the whole utterance, part of the whole thing. So to my mind, 'communication' is a rather misleading word to say that's what's going on.

# Questions for Discussion:

*1. Would you be interested in translating novels if you had sufficient command of another language? Why or why not?*

*2. Why do you think that David is so rarely in a position to defend Noam Chomsky and his views on linguistics?*

*3. Has this chapter increased your desire to read "Life: A User's Manual" or any other work by Georges Perec?*

## II. An Illustrative Capture

*Learning from The Great Escape*

**HB**: In your book, you give this wonderful example of a scene from the movie *The Great Escape*, when two characters have escaped their prisoner of war camp and they're having their papers checked by the authorities before boarding a bus. One of them is German-speaking and the other one isn't, and they are just about to get past the German guard when the guard turns to them and says *"Good luck!"* in English. The one who is not a German speaker turns back and says *"Thank you!"* which gets them caught.

You point out that one of the interesting things about this example is that it makes no difference what they are actually saying to one another. The exchange could have been: *"Have a nice day"* and *"Thank you"*, or *"Your shoes are untied"* and *"No, they're not"*.

This seems an extreme example of some of the challenges that must occur in translation, in terms of context.

**DB**: Yes, it's a rather extreme demonstration of the difference between the meaning of *what is said* and the meaning of *it having been said.* In the case of the policeman who is not supposed to understand English but reveals that he does, it's not what he said that's important, it's that it was said *in English.*

As a result, if you switch off the sound track and just look at that sequence in the movie it is totally incomprehensible. If you switch off the screen and just hear the soundtrack: somebody says *"Good luck"*, somebody else says, *"Thank you"*. So what?

I would also like to add something here that I didn't know about when I wrote my book, but I do know now, because the book has been translated into Spanish and I've had a long interaction with my Spanish translator on this. *The Great Escape,* obviously, has been dubbed into Spanish and viewed many times in Spain and South America, and in the Spanish dubbing of it the German policeman and the non-German speaking English escapee say *"Good luck"* and *"Thank you"* to one another *in Spanish.*

How is this possible? I mean, these are not Spanish escapees, and the German police don't speak Spanish. How is it possible?

My translator Vicente Campos González, who is an absolutely wonderful guy, explained to me that there is a convention within the Spanish language world that in World War II movies, Germans speak German but the Allies speak Spanish. That is to say, Spanish is taken to be, is understood as, English.

**HB**: Or perhaps French, I suppose, depending on the context.

**DB**: Yes, that's right. The language barrier is between Spanish representing all other languages and German representing German. So that it's perfectly comprehensible in Spanish, even though the Englishness of it is not revealed, because the Spanish soundtrack is taken to represent English.

**HB**: They just make that link automatically.

**DB**: Yes. So that's something I didn't know. It shows the extraordinary flexibility and variability and cultural specificity of these kinds of things. We can do all sorts of things with language that seem to be implausible and impossible, but we can do them.

# Questions for Discussion:

*1. How might one go about translating, in written form, the bus capture scene from* **The Great Escape** *in a third language, like Hungarian?*

*2. To what extent does this chapter shed light on the tendency for German characters to speak English with a strong German accent in American and British WWII films?*

# III. Getting the Joke

*Translating humour*

**HB**: You don't just talk about translation in a theoretical context but rather from the perspective of someone actively engaged in the practical task of actually doing translations. One gets a sense that there are no hard and fast rules; instead, you convey a sense of working with something, playing with something, trying it out and seeing what happens on a case-by-case basis.

In particular, two things that certainly struck me as potentially great challenges for a translator were how best to convey the personal style of an author and how best to convey humour. In particular, humour is something that a lot of people may think: *Well, that surely can't be done. You can't convey a pun as you move from one language to another.* There is this sense that humour necessarily gets lost in translation.

But you give tangible demonstrations to the contrary, showing that, in fact, you can translate humour meaningfully. You have to think about it and work hard, but there are definitely ways of doing it. In fact, one gets a sense that that's part and parcel of what a good translator actually does: rolling up one's sleeves and working as long as it takes to be able to find this right match. And when it comes to humour, you give a few specific examples of how this can be done. But still, I imagine that it's very difficult to come up with those.

**DB**: It's like everything: it seems impossible until you've done it. Then it seems quite easy, retrospectively—you can't quite recall how long it took. But other times it just comes to you.

**HB**: Would you say that humour is one of the hardest things to translate?

**DB**: I don't like these categorizations of what's hard or what's easy. I'm doing a translation course, a very practical translation course, with some senior students at Princeton this semester. We're working with texts of very different kinds (I insist on them doing very different kinds of things): bits of advertisements, bits of journalism, fine bits of writing from novels and high literature, and non-fiction stuff. Some is very well written, some not very well written. It isn't true that anything is easier or harder than anything else. They all have their specific types of problems that you have to get your mind around. When you get into the run of it, you can become a good and fluent translator of journalistic prose, but that's because you're learning to write journalistic prose in English.

So, no, I don't like those scales of what's hard and what's easy. Everything and anything may at some random point suddenly become very difficult, but I wouldn't generalize.

Humour, on the other hand, is a special case, but it's not as special as most people make out. Humour is a very broad thing—there are many kinds of humour—but it's also a very fragile thing. There are lots of jokes that I make that my granddaughter doesn't get, even in the same language. So why *should* a joke travel from A to B, because it's never guaranteed of being received even in its own language?

**HB**: And, of course, one may get it and still not think it's funny.

**DB**: Absolutely, that's right. So it's very fragile. And there are many types of humour: slapstick humour, physical humour, scatological humour, funny stories about the Belgians that are, for the French, exactly the same as British stories about the Irish, or Swedish stories about Finns, which are very similar and you can do in any language.

There are lots of kinds of humorous anecdotes and joke structures that are eminently transportable, where their linguistic texture isn't nearly as important as the deceptions that they involve, or their timing and surprise effects. All that kind of humour is neither easier nor more difficult to translate than a story.

What it boils down to, when you want to talk about really interesting translation challenges, are obviously humorous and other forms of expression that refer back to themselves: they actually use the words of which they are made as the focus or the turning point. There you have to be quite imaginative: you have to jump, as it were, and transpose and find something that will turn in a similar way, but obviously it has to turn on something else, because the particular word that's being punned on is not present in the translation.

**HB**: You mention one in particular in your book. It was, if I recall, a sign—

**DB**: Yes, that's right—an unapologetically chosen example from one of my own translations of Perec: a joke visiting card that said *"Adolf Hitler, Fourreur"*, which is the French word for furrier, but also the way the French would pronounce 'Führer'.

And I turned that into *"Adolf Hitler, German Lieder"*. OK, it's not the greatest joke in the world, but it works, it does the job.

The translations by Anthea Bell of the comic strip cartoon *Astérix* into English are full of inventions far better than mine. She has a wonderful ability—in that very constrained format of the comic strip, because you don't have much room there—to find something that is a good joke in English that will stand in lieu of a good joke in French.

You could say that those things are translators' nightmares, but actually they're not. They're the translator's cherry: they're the fun bits. Because when you get them, you feel so pleased with yourself. And when you don't, of course, either the entire text becomes pointless—if it hangs solely on a joke—or nobody notices.

# Questions for Discussion:

*1. Are you surprised by David's view that, in general, humour is no easier or no more difficult than any other aspect of translation?*

*2. Do good translators necessarily need to have good sense of humour?*

# IV. Probing the Foreign

*Dickens, word order, and Anglo-Italian gibberish*

**DB**: There is a nice little speculation—I've speculated with other people on this recently and I still don't know the answer to it— regarding the English literary tradition that prides itself on its comic dimension. The British and Americans are very good at comedy in literature, at integrating comicalness into high writing, from Shakespeare onwards. And there's this sense that the French and German traditions are altogether more serious: you don't go to French literature or German literature to have a laugh.

Now, this is possibly an effect of translation—that translated literature is, by and large, just a few degrees less humorous than the original. Do you see what I mean? The argument may actually be entirely circular, with English literature being neither funnier, nor less funny, than any other literature: you're just reading it in the original, while with non-English literature you're not getting the jokes. In fact, I think what's much more difficult or delicate or tricky in this field is not so much actual jokes you can isolate—you know, funny anecdotes—but humorousness in general.

I've been reading *Martin Chuzzlewit* recently, which is Dickens' funniest novel. You can't really put your finger on it and say, *"That's the funny bit right there."* But there's a sense of playfulness with language, entertaining you with the oddities of the English language, all the way through. It's that kind of semi-self-referential, semi-metalinguistic lightness of touch that you can never be sure you've really got across into another language.

**HB**: And presumably you have to have an extremely deep awareness of all the subtleties of the language to be able to bring that out.

**DB**: You have to have a judgment of where that lies; and of course people's judgments may vary as to how funny Dickens is. I'm sure my granddaughter doesn't find him funny at all.

**HB**: You're picking on your poor granddaughter quite a bit. She doesn't seem to find anything funny.

**DB**: I am very fond of her, but of course I am just using her as an example: even when people know each other quite well there are huge differences in what is funny and what is not. So in the public reading of a piece of literary fiction, the responses will vary quite substantially, and the translator has to make a choice as to where to pitch that. It's not surprising if most translators pitch it, as it were, a notch or two below, because the one thing you don't want to do is to make it seem ridiculous. You don't want to overdo the comedy.

So, maybe the idea that the British literary tradition is particularly marked by its talent for comedy is really just a secondary reflection of the unawareness that people have that Tolstoy and Chekhov and Cervantes didn't write in English.

**HB**: You talk about how some people actually want to have foreignness when they pick up a translation, but to be able to appreciate foreignness the irony is that you have to have some familiarity with the culture itself. You make this joke about German...

**DB**: Yes. *"To understand this is a translation from German, you have to recognize that German sentences at the end of their clauses their main verbs leave."*

**HB**: Exactly. Which means that you have to recognize German word order in advance. Otherwise it's not funny.

**DB**: Yes. Then it's just bad.

**HB**: Or it's not recognizable. It's difficult for you to recognize that something is typically Zulu, if you don't know anything about Zulu.

**DB**: Well, that's something that I rather expected to have a big argument about with other people, but it hasn't really happened yet, so I'll have that argument with myself.

It depends on your interpretation, but if a book is presented to you through its jacket and the blurb around it as a great new work in English from Outer Ruritania that gives us some authentic expression of Ruritanian world view, and you find that the English is slightly odd, then you will interpret that as Ruritanianness. You can be told what it is that you are learning.

And of course nobody ever reads anything in a complete vacuum. Things do arrive with a surrounding aura. I think I could argue against myself there and say: *"On the contrary, especially in English, which is a language of so many different dialects and varieties, many novelists do effectively teach us what it is like to be Nigerian or South African and you do learn; it can be a learning experience."*

There is a to and fro between languages that can happen through the vector of literature that can be enriching in English. But I suppose it all comes down to the fact that a written text on its own tells us very little about where it comes from. You have to know something before you can do any of this interpretation.

**HB**: Again, it's this whole context or meta-context or what have you. When discussing this whole question about foreignness, I really must mention something else you mentioned in your book. There's a hilarious clip of this Italian fellow Adriano Celantano, where he's singing what is supposed to be an English pop song with girls dancing around, but it's not actually in English at all: it's just babble.

**DB**: Yes. It sounds perfectly likely. It's phonetically perfect. It's linguistically and intellectually a very interesting little act, in that it shows that you can use the phonemes of Italian to mimic the phonemic structure of English without speaking English. Of course the whole point would be lost if it were in English. The transcription of those lyrics in Italian—of course they're meaningless in Italian as well— just happens to be those that, when pronounced aloud in Italian, sound like English.

In theory, languages have different phonemic structures: they sound different, they use different sounds. But of course they overlap—some sounds are familiar—and it is extraordinarily clever to pick exactly those sounds of Italian that can masquerade as sounds of English. It's not given to everybody to find the path that will allow you to do that. So what does that prove? That proves that you can sound foreign by not saying anything at all if you are good at making foreign sounds out of your own linguistic resources.

## Questions for Discussion:

*1. Do you share David's instincts that all languages might be "equally suited towards the comic"?*

*2. Compare the effects of Adriano Celantano's gibberish song with that of Charlie Chaplin's famous scene at the end of **Modern Times**.*

# V. Films in Translation

*Subtitles, dubbing, and "The Bergman Effect"*

**HB**: You mentioned constraints before when talking about cartoons and Anthea Bell, but another spatial constraint you mentioned in your book had to do with subtitles. You talk about something called The Bergman Effect, whereby the director actually tempers the film he's creating to fit the constraints of future subtitles.

**DB**: Maybe not so explicitly, but they are just simply aware that you can't put too much language on the screen, because if it's going to be circulated internationally through the medium of subtitling, and if the dialogue is all-important, then you've got to spread it out. Who knows if The Bergman Effect actually exists, but it's a hypothesis that goes as follows:

The image we have of Swedes as people who are seriously verbally-challenged depressives is actually a product of the fact that almost anything people have seen of Sweden are Bergman's movies, and that Bergman made movies for the international market—for artistic, not so much commercial reasons—in such a way that the whole film can be seen in such a way where you can't have too much language going on in any one sequence, otherwise you wouldn't be able to fit it in the subtitle.

With another class just we were looking at *Slumdog Millionaire*, that amazing movie set in Mumbai, which is itself linguistically very hybrid because it's part Hindi and part English.

We were looking at the Spanish subtitled version of it. The French did a dubbed version where everybody just speaks perfect French all the way through (no Hindi or English). That flattens the movie very considerably, because you get a lot of information from the voice track.

In the Spanish version, you've still got that voice track, but you've got Spanish subtitles. We did notice how cleverly the film is done in the way that it cuts from sequence to sequence. There is enough room to put pretty much all the dialogue into subtitles. That's part of the film director's art of editing, using sounds and noises as well to fill in gaps between speech.

Maybe we shouldn't call it "The Bergman Effect." Maybe we should just recognize it as the common sense of the makers of movies who need an international audience, knowing that one of the constraints on their art is not to overload the dialogue in dense patches because that will necessarily limit the effect.

**HB**: Just one final point on Bergman that you had mentioned that I thought was pretty funny. The claim is that when he is making movies for a domestic audience he naturally doesn't worry about this at all, and that has a substantial effect on the types of films that he makes: they tend to have more dialogue, they're chattier.

**DB**: And much jollier. Yes, yes.

**HB**: Which is not something that, as you said before, people would naturally associate with Bergman or Swedes in general through Bergman's work.

**DB**: That's right.

# Questions for Discussion:

*1. What does David mean, exactly, when he says that the French dubbed version of* **Slumdog Millionaire** *"flattens the movie considerably because you get a lot of information from the voice track"?*

*2. Do you prefer to watch movies that are dubbed or in the original with subtitles? Does this chapter help you understand your preferences?*

# VI. The Varieties of English

*In search of a middle form*

**HB**: Getting back to translation. Clearly a translator is an active participant in the process, to the extent that when you come out with a translation it's also your work. It's a translation, but it's also your work, and presumably it's done in the Bellos style. So it's a faithful reproduction in English from some French author, but it is also a work by yourself.

**DB**: Yes, I wrote it.

**HB**: Has your style as a writer, as a translator, changed in the years that you've been translating? And if so, how?

**DB**: That's not a judgment for me to make. If anybody is interested in 20 years' time they could do a stylometric analysis of the entire output...

**HB**: OK, but does it feel different for you? When it comes to translation, do you feel that you are doing things differently now compared to before?

**DB**: No. I certainly feel more confident now than I did 25 years ago, that what I write is going to be OK, but that's just the effect of experience and getting older.

It's a dialogic experience, it goes two ways. I'm sure that my command of the English language and my ability to write has been formed by all these foreign writers that I've had to translate. They've made me learn different things and different nooks and crannies of English.

The book called *On Leave* by Daniel Anselme (original title *La Permission*) that I translated is set in the 1950s, which is when I was a little boy. I can't remember what army slang in the 1950s was—I wasn't in the army—so I had to go and look it up. I've had to educate myself and constantly reassess. And, of course, I can't get it *completely* right. My only hope is that there is nobody actually left who was in the army in the 1950s. But it needs to sound *now* like 1950s army slang.

And that may be a little different, which is one of the reasons why the question of authenticity that people raise so often really irritates me. The true authenticity of what conscripts in the Algerian War would have sounded like in 1956 had they been soldiers in the British or American Army seems to me a completely pointless question. You can't know that. You can't ever know. But what you *can* do is try to simulate something that will summon up images of the language of soldiers of the 1950s.

**HB**: For the people now.

**DB**: Yes, that's right: for the people now. I suppose what has happened through the history of the books that I've translated and the publishers I've translated them for, and also through my transposition from Britain to the United States, is that I'm much more aware now of the varieties of English—of the multiplicity of "Englishes"—and of the difficulty of finding a middle form, a central form of the English language that is neither American nor British but would be taken as both.

**HB**: This is the "Tranglish" you wrote about.

**DB**: Yes, 'Tranglish'. It is a stylistic feat. Years ago, when I started translating Perec, it was just obvious to me to translate into English. *I know what English is. English is what I write.*

But 25 years later, I don't know what English is anymore. I'm much less sure of my ground in saying, *"This is English and this isn't"* or *"This is good English or this isn't"*, or even, indeed, *"This is British and this is American"*, because there are all sorts of strange crossovers.

It comes down to little details, and I'm very, very glad to have had the services of copy editors on both sides of the Atlantic who've helped me a lot with that: producing texts that are readable and enjoyable without causing offense or being incomprehensible.

Sometimes you just have to make a choice: it's either British or American, or European or American. Take the floors of a house. You can't be ambiguous about the ground floor and the first floor: there is no term that can encompass them both. There are some things where it either has to be European or has to be American, but there is a very substantial range of expression and style where you can, with a bit of craft, put it in the middle, so that it works both ways without being completely colourless.

That is a problem of translation into English that doesn't exist into French. Obviously there are many varieties of French, but there is a much stronger concept of what the central language is and how a thing should be written.

**HB**: Well, you have an *Académie française*, of course, and you don't have the counterpart in English.

**DB**: That's right.

# Questions for Discussion:

*1. Are there disadvantages to looking for a "middle form" of English?*

*2. Do you agree with David that "you can't ever know" what conscripts in the Algerian War would have sounded like in 1956 had they been British or American soldiers? How might one argue against this view?*

# VII. Asserting Our Individuality

*Language as an expression of our identity*

**HB**: I'm going to switch gears now and ask you a different sort of question that you might have seen coming: why don't we all speak one language?

**DB**: The answer to that is because we don't want to. And I'm actually quite sure of this.

As we all know, any human infant can learn to speak any human language. And we all know that there is nothing genetic about this. It's not because you are born to a Chinese mother that you are predisposed to speaking Chinese. There is some argument about where the process of language learning begins, and some people would maintain that it does actually begin in the womb, but that doesn't really matter to my argument because even if it begins in the womb it is still the result of external stimuli.

So, the language that you learn is the product of external stimuli—that's to say the environment in which you're born—and there is no more reason for you to learn Chinese than to learn English and vice versa. It depends where you start. The human language faculty is capable of generating and producing and living in any language. There is no destiny about it, there is no fatality about it. There is absolutely nothing genetic about it.

That's point one.

**HB**: I think that's universally agreed upon.

**DB**: Yes, but people don't necessarily go on to the next step of thinking about this, which is: *But* we all speak different languages. We *could* all speak any language, but we all speak differently.

Moreover, within a given thing that we call 'language', actually everybody speaks differently: socially, regionally, down to clan, street gang, family.

*"Yes, yes"*, you can say, *"This is a natural process of dialect,"* or whatever. But then look even closer: apart from the distinction in pitch of voice in adults between male and female voices, which is physiological (though even there, there's a considerable overlap), but apart from that, there's no reason why in the same family, say, we shouldn't all speak *exactly* the same. Because we all have the same external stimuli, we talk to each other. Yet we don't.

When I ring my sister up on the phone, she says *"Hello, brother".* She knows who it is, amongst the thousands of male voices she's heard. And you might say, *"Oh, well, that's the body, that's just physio-logical,"* but it isn't actually, because we know that if you want to, you can talk exactly like someone else.

Meryl Streep is absolutely Margaret Thatcher in *The Iron Lady.* If you train yourself, if you make the effort, all of us can be Meryl Streeps. But we don't. Why? Because we don't want to.

Think about it: how useful would language be if we *did* sound alike? If Uncle Jim and Aunty Josie sounded the same when they were calling to you in the dark, you wouldn't know which was which.

Deep down at the very bottom of "what language is for," it's obvious to me that human speech is a form of self-identification, and that accounts for this very obvious fact that we not only don't bother to speak like our parents, sisters, brothers and neighbours, we *deliberately* develop a form of diction that identifies us: me as me and you as you, whilst also signalling a particular identity.

Sometimes we signal this down to a very, very fine geographical or social identity, sometimes a very broad one. But always when we speak, whatever we say about our social or regional or geographic origins, we are also saying to people whose social and geographic origins are identical: *"It's **me**, not **you**, who is speaking here."*

**HB**: At all different levels, it seems. There is the personal level of us identifying ourselves within the family, as you said before, but this also works, as you mentioned, at a community level and beyond.

**DB**: Yes, distinguishing one group from the other. So, if the only way we think about language is as a means of communication, as you were saying around half an hour ago, well, all this would be completely useless and pointless. Language would be a totally different kind of thing if it were just a mode of communication.

Just imagine if none of our voices could be distinguished from each other. We'd have to live in a totally different way. It would be quite nice to do a sort of TV reality show about this, actually.

**HB**: Reality shows never seem to have anything to do with reality.

**DB**: No, they don't.

**HB**: This one also wouldn't either. It would be a hypothesis show.

**DB**: Yes, this, too, would indeed be an unreality show, but you could do it now with technology: have people speaking to each other when you cannot distinguish which voice was which. What would they have to do to live in a house together? It would be something different from the kind of human relations and social relations that we now have.

**HB**: Perhaps they would do more exaggerated things with their body language, with the way they held themselves, as a way of distinguishing themselves, in keeping with what you've just been saying.

**DB**: I don't know. Maybe we'd just have totally different kinds of human relations, a different kind of society.

This is a very simple argument for saying that it is in the nature of language to be different. The other trend, the push towards making language the same—standard languages, written languages—is another dimension of our social organization and cultural lives, and the two are in permanent tension.

Translation is in the middle between these two things. It represents these two tensions of being completely unique and of being sharable. And that's why it's so interesting.

But it really does annoy me when people say, *"Oh, it is terribly simple. Translation just takes the meaning from here to there."* It's not quite so simple.

## Questions for Discussion:

*1. Do you agree with David that we deliberately use language as a means of asserting our identity?*

*2. What do you think would happen if we were to construct the "Reality TV Show" that David mentions in this chapter?*

# VIII. Translation and Meaning

*Extending the Principle of Effability*

**HB**: You say in your book that in order to understand what the meaning of something is, you sometimes actually have to translate it. So, there is a certain sense that the translation is the meaning.

**DB**: Well, I stick my neck out even further. I say that—not sometimes but in the last analysis—the only way of truly asserting that something has meaning is to provide a translation of it. Because that is the test of meaningfulness: if it is translatable, it is meaningful. If it's not translatable, it must always be questionable as to whether it has any meaning or not.

**HB**: I wanted to get to that, because to me that was an interesting and somewhat provocative idea. I don't know if this is a common view or more your own particular take on things. Perhaps I should just ask you that to start with: is the view that you're enunciating now one that most people would hold in the world of translation, or is that more your own thing?

**DB**: You know, I sometimes forget where I pick up my ideas. Particularly in this translation book, I know I have used all sorts of things that have come to me over the years from here, there and everywhere.

I haven't always been able to track back exactly where I first heard that. But the idea of translatability as the validation of meaning, I have found or refound in the philosophy of Donald Davidson. But he's a very difficult person to read. And his commentator, an Australian philosopher, J.E. Malpas, is the person I read on this.

But I think the idea has a much longer history than that, but I'm not an expert in philosophy. I think that the idea that meaning has to be validated—to say that something has meaning can't just be taken as a given, and that one test for meaningfulness is the possibility of transcribing it into some other symbolic system—I think that's a 20th-century English philosophy idea rather than an ancient Greek idea. The ancient Greeks didn't think in those terms at all because everything was in Greek anyways.

I probably picked it up when I was a very young man at Oxford, being surrounded by the clouds of Oxford philosophy that were going on. But wherever it comes from, it seems to me a very important idea, if only because it allows you to grapple with one of those other nostrums or clichés that are always thrown about in this field, about the untranslatable.

Just what can you possibly mean by an untranslatable word or sentence or something like that? Because if it truly were untranslatable, there would be nothing you could say about it.

So how can you possibly know? The logic of the arguments about the untranslatable and the ineffable irritate me greatly.

**HB**: OK, I'd love to explore your irritation, so let me see if I can get a sense of things. There is this thing that you mention in your book called 'the axiom of...

**DB**: 'The axiom of effability', yes. The basic idea is that we take language as having the capacity or the potential to express anything and everything that human beings might want to express, and insofar as something is not expressible, it is not within the field of language.

**HB**: So, anything that I can think of, I can express in language?

**DB**: Yes.

**HB**: Any thought that I have, I can express in language?

**DB**: Any thought, any feeling, any state that a human can have, can be expressed in a human language.

**HB**: My recollection is that the syllogism then goes on to say: any language can be translated into any other language. Right?

**DB**: Well, that's the part I said: what can be said in any language can be said in any other. Because otherwise you would have to presuppose that there were different kinds of human beings: that a Chinese person thinks Chinese thoughts or an English person has English thoughts, feelings and states. And I won't have that. Because there's no evidence for it at all.

## Questions for Discussion:

*1. Do you agree with David's claim that the only way of truly asserting that something has meaning is to provide a translation of it?*

*2. Might it be possible to "translate" gibberish, such as Adriano Celantano's pseudo-English song mentioned in Chapter 4? If so, what, if anything does that imply for David's claim in the question above?*

# IX. Mathematics and Music

*Pushing the boundaries of "language-like"*

**HB**: This brings up two questions that I'd like to ask you. The first involves this sense of linguistic equivalence that you just mentioned. Then I'd like to explore the idea of how language might structure our thoughts, and whether or not we would somehow think differently if we spoke a different language. You mentioned this a little bit in your book when you talked about the notion of a "Platonic Hopi".

But let me first go back to my other question. We've just said that any thought I have can be expressed in a language, while you claim that if I express it in one language, I can express it in another.

But what if I'm a mathematician and I'm thinking about some theorem that I naturally express in mathematics. And when some English speaker who doesn't know mathematics asks me about it, I try to explain it to her: I give metaphors and roundabout descriptions of what's going on, but I know that I'm not really getting to the heart of things: I'm just giving some kind of loose description.

**DB**: Yes: that's not the real thing.

**HB**: Right.

**DB**: The real thing is in math.

**HB**: Exactly. So what's going on? I had a thought and I've expressed it in a language, and the language that I'm using is mathematics.

**DB**: Mathematics is not a language. Mathematics is mathematics. We don't need to say what it is: it is math.

**HB**: But if it's not a language then...

**DB**: Just as music is not language either: music is music. It's a wonderful, complex thing that human beings can do, but you can no more translate music into English prose than you can translate the language of ants into English prose, because they are different things.

**HB**: OK, so it's not a language, then....

**DB**: Or that it's not language in the important sense that I want to deal with. Sure, it's something that can express thought. Mathematics does express thought. And within mathematics, there is always more than one mathematical way of writing some proposition or theorem. Mathematics rewrites itself all the time.

But it's not useful for the purposes of our discussion to try to include formal symbolic things like math or expressive symbolic things like music or painting or dance or all these generically different things, or even the rustling of the trees and the noise cars make. They are not, interestingly, language.

**HB**: But wasn't the first part of this that any thought I have could be expressed in a language? So then if math or music isn't actually a language, then aren't those somehow thoughts that can't be expressed in a language? I mean, once things are expressed in a language, I'll grant you that you can map them to another one, which is your claim. But haven't I just given examples of things I've thought of that somehow can't be expressed in a language?

**DB**: Well, I guess that's a job for cognitive science people to come up with a convincing answer for.

**HB**: But what do you think? What is your feeling about that?

**DB**: I think the Principle of Effability does run up against this problem, but there are many human mental activities that result in things that look like expressions—and indeed, you call them mathematical expressions or musical expressions. But to my mind, they are radically different from those things that are expressed in language, radically different because they exist in a different medium, a different mode. I don't think that really undermines the Principle of Effability.

I don't want to say that music is ineffable because we can't say what it means. It's just music. It's something different. There is no earthly reason why these other forms of cultural activity should be transmutable the one into the other. But language can cover all the needs that we wish to make of it.

So, there is nothing language-like that we can think or formulate that cannot be expressed in a language. And what can be expressed in a language can always be expressed in any language.

I suppose it pushes back the boundary of...

**HB**: ...what we mean by 'language-like'.

**DB**: Yes. There is a degree of circularity about the definition.

## Questions for Discussion:

*1. Do you agree or disagree with the Principle of Effability?*

*2. Is mathematics a language?*

# X. Language and Thought

*Plato, Hopi, and jumping mind-grooves*

**HB**: OK, let me move on now to talk about this idea of a Platonic Hopi, which has been on my mind of late. You obviously find deeply repellent any notion of cultural hierarchy like we had in the days of the British Empire: *We are civilized people who think in a superior way and we use the superior language, while there are these peons, colonials, what have you, who can't possibly be able to think our high enlightened thoughts because they don't have the right language.*

**DB**: Not only that: *We have to send them to school and teach them to think properly.*

**HB**: Right. There is a clear sense that I get from reading your book and our discussion today of your passionate egalitarianism: not political correctness, but an overriding belief in the universality of the human condition and the enormous power, the liberating power, that translation serves to be able to connect one group of people to those who live in a very different linguistic and cultural milieu.

And yet, when I think of this example of the Native American Hopi and Plato...

**DB**: Well, I borrowed the example of Hopi from Benjamin Whorf who made it famous. Everybody quotes him and not always correctly. I just tried to use the story about Hopi evidentials as an illustration.

**HB**: OK. Well, my understanding is that, in the Hopi language, "the farmer killed the duck" is a sentence that can't be said in an unambiguous way.

**DB**: It can be said in Hopi, but you have to add something, because you have to know whether the farmer is present, not present, or only a matter of report, because the grammatical form of the word has to be in one of those three cases. There are a couple of dozen languages around the world that do this, that mark the evidential status on the noun.

The farmer I can see has a different grammatical form from the farmer I can't see. There is a third grammatical form for the farmer you told me about, and similarly for the duck. So, you can't translate "the farmer killed the duck," that set of information, into Hopi without adding some additional information. The English sentence just doesn't give you enough information to say anything in Hopi.

**HB**: Presumably then, from a Hopi perspective, that means that, linguistically, there's no abstract sense of 'duck'. There's the duck that's here, there's the duck that was over there, there's the duck that I can't see, there's the duck...

**DB**: No actually.

**HB**: That's not right?

**DB**: Well, I don't think so. Because look: in Latin, you can't say the word 'man' just like that, because it has to be either in the nominative, accusative, genitive, dative or ablative case. You can't generalize and say there is therefore no concept of 'man' because you've got six separate cases. No, I think that's a step too far, jumping too far. You're trying to make Hopi conform to an English concept of what a thing is. There is no reason you should.

**HB**: Well, I'm really trying to understand whether it can conform to an ancient Greek sense, because I want to get to this question of whether or not there could have been a Platonic Hopi. And sadly, I don't speak Greek either. But my sense is—and you mentioned this yourself in your book—that because of the structure of the language, had Plato been writing in Hopi...

**DB**: ...he probably would have thought different thoughts.

**HB**: And so there is the claim that we would not have had Platonic philosophy had Plato been raised in Hopi. So, if left up to the Hopis, you don't get Platonic philosophy. Now maybe this is a good thing, maybe it's a bad thing, but it's a thing.

**DB**: Yes. We need to have a balanced view. Again, as in so many of the other things you've asked me about today, I see this more as a matter of tensions and dialogue and movement back and forth.

There was an argument made by Edward Sapir, who was one of Whorf's colleagues but also a far more important thinker. Whorf was a great linguist of American native languages and came out with lots and lots of material. Sapir was much broader.

Sapir's point is not that the grammar of the language that you speak imprisons your mind in particular ways of thinking, but that it does actually incline you in certain directions, that some things are easier than others, as they are repeated and therefore reinforced all the time.

In English, we always have to distinguish between the definite and the indefinite, and no doubt that inclines us to philosophical views in which that distinction is important, because it's just easier to say. Greek and Latin and the languages derived from them have devices within them that make it easy to jump from a verb to an abstract quantity. You can jump from a noun to an abstract quantity, you can jump from an adjective to an abstract quantity.

From *This man is just*, you can easily invent the word *justice*, the quality that a just man has. English has inherited this from the classical languages like many other languages have, just as we add "ness" to something to form a describing word for the quality that is granted. That structure is not necessarily the structure of the world, but it makes speakers of those languages inclined to describe the world in those terms, because it's easy.

**HB**: You use the expression "mind grooves".

**DB**: Yes: these grooves that are dug again and again, reinforced by the language that you use. The question is: *can you jump from one groove to another?*

**HB**: Is it possible?

**DB**: Yes, is it possible? That is the question. The question isn't really: *"Why didn't Plato write in a Native American language?"* In a sense that's a silly question, a slightly offensive question as well.

**HB**: *Could the Hopi actually understand and recognize Platonic philosophy?* Isn't that really the question?

**DB**: I'd rather put the question the other way around: if you are a speaker of Greek or English or French or Latin, you are peculiarly ill-equipped to understand Hopi philosophy.

**HB**: Well, sure, they're equivalent. They're completely symmetric. This is not a statement about cultural hierarchy. It is about the connection between language and thought.

**DB**: Now, *ill-equipped* is one thing, but *impossible* is another. I'm very reluctant to say anything is impossible. How could you know that it's impossible? All you can say is, *Well, it hasn't been done.* The conditions for claiming that something like this is impossible seem to me to be very hard to meet. You have to be very, very sure of something to say it's impossible. And obviously it can't be true that you can never jump from one mind groove to another, because if it were you couldn't know it. I couldn't have explained to you the difference of Hopi from the Indo-European language structures if the Indo-European language that I speak, namely English, didn't allow me to imagine another one.

**HB**: OK, but it's possible that you can jump from some mind grooves to another, but not from *all* mind grooves to another.

**DB**: That's possible. But let's take the example that many people will find more familiar: the difference between languages with grammatical gender and languages without. Now, English doesn't have a grammatical gender.

**HB**: Thank goodness.

**DB**: Exactly. All English-language speakers find mastery of the grammatical gender system of, say, French or German or Spanish boring, burdensome, mind-boggling, and you're never sure that you've got it right 100% of the time.

And the question arises: is there some fundamental difference between being brought up as a speaker of French such that the issue of *what gender is this?* never arises, because *you just know?* Can you ever really transit from that state to the other state? Can I, as a life-long learner of French, ever really have gender language in the full, natural sense that a French person has?

I don't know the answer to that, because, actually, the French *do* make mistakes sometimes themselves. I don't know whether my grasp of gender is identical to or slightly different from that of my wife, who was brought up in French. I don't quite know what form of testing could be carried out, or where you could stand in order to judge that difference.

That's the problem of saying, *X could never be expressed in Y.* It presupposes Z, the position from which you can judge the difference or similarity. And that's very hard: it requires being in some supra-linguistic cloud in the sky, and you can only ever be in one language or another.

Also, I should say that everything is ideological and personal, as well as intellectual and general. I also don't want it to be true that there are people who can think thoughts that by definition I will never be able to understand, because I wasn't exposed to their language at a critical age. That's not a hopeful position to adopt.

**HB**: So this is linked to the conviction that, with enough effort, under the right circumstances, all human knowledge and all human thinking is accessible to you.

**DB**: Yes. The contrary is paradoxical. It has to be nonsense. Because how can I assert that there are people over there whom I will never understand? How would I know that? It's like you're boxing yourself in with a kind of a brick wall. You couldn't ever know that you were right.

**HB**: But you might be. It's possible.

**DB**: No. It might be incidentally the case that I will never get to understand them because life is short and I spend my time doing other things. But to claim that, in principle, there are little green men on Mars who have thoughts and communicate them to each other, but I will never be able to know what they are—well, that's an unacceptable position for all sorts of human reasons. It may have turned out that we never cracked Linear B, and it may have turned out that we never did crack hieroglyphs...

**HB**: ...but that doesn't mean that, in principle, they're un-crackable.

**DB**: Exactly.

## Questions for Discussion:

*1. Do you think that you'd have different thoughts if you were raised in a different culture and language?*

*2. To what extent is it appropriate for one's egalitarian beliefs to influence one's views on language and thought?*

# XI. Paying Respects

*Valuing the translators in our midst*

**HB**: Well, this has been a fascinating conversation for me, David. Is there anything I haven't asked that you would like to mention? Anything you'd like to highlight or emphasize before we conclude?

**DB**: Well, there are some things in my book that are perhaps not developed enough, and there are some things I've left out that I hope other people will write about too.

**HB**: Do you have plans to write more about these topics, based upon the response, the voluminous mailbags, that you've received? Are you thinking more about another book?

**DB**: I'm thinking about another book, but not about translation. I'm thinking about a book about fiction, about reading fiction.

But to answer your last question, I do, throughout the book, take a generally positive and encouraging attitude towards the people who do translations, but I don't go on particularly about how badly they're paid and how badly they're treated, because there are plenty of other books that do that. But it is true that they are badly paid and badly treated.

What we haven't talked about in this conversation is that I really do think that—especially in the English-speaking world—people should just stop for a minute and think how much they gain from translators. They do jobs that are not very glamorous, but really necessary and worthwhile. I think it would be nice if a greater proportion of people in the English-speaking world thought just a little bit more about all that goes into the world they live in that depends on, or is channelled through, people who work as translators.

The people I don't speak about in my book, out of ignorance and not out of unwillingness, are the many, often volunteers, who work in courts and in hospitals in what's called community interpreting. These are often life-and-death situations, where all the difficulties of translation that I talk about in the book are present, plus others: like being responsible for communication between a dying patient and a doctor or getting somebody convicted or off. These are real heroes.

And they're quite numerous, because there are an awful lot of linguistic minorities in the US and in the UK, and they have rights as linguistic minorities to have interpreter services.

It seems to me important that significant resources should be provided, not only to make these translators' lives moderately comfortable, but also to support them both psychologically and humanly. They are doing really stressful, burdensome, painful jobs, and they deserve a lot more recognition, visibility and support than they currently get.

**HB**: Hopefully they will start to get it. And hopefully more people in the English-speaking world will also begin to read more books in translation. As I mentioned earlier this morning before we started this conversation, my personal sense as a consumer of books is that more and more works of literature penned in languages other than English are now becoming available in translation. Hopefully that trend will continue, if not actually in fact increase.

**DB**: I sincerely hope so too, and I hope to contribute to it.

**HB**: Well, you already have. Thank you very much for your time, David. It's been a great pleasure talking to you.

**DB**: Thank you, Howard.

# Questions for Discussion:

*1. Does this chapter make you more sensitive to the important role that translators play in our society?*

*2. Has this conversation influenced your willingness to read works in translation?*

## Continuing the Conversation

Readers are encouraged to read David's book, *Is That a Fish In Your Ear: Translation and the Meaning of Everything* which goes into considerable additional detail about many of the issues discussed here.

# Sign Language Linguistics

A conversation with Carol Padden

# Introduction

*Heeding the Signs*

What makes a language a language?

Simple, right? Any time a group of humans get together and use a collectively-recognized series of utterances to successfully communicate ideas and concepts, we've got ourselves a language.

Well, sort of.

What if I gesture to a stranger in a distant land about locally available food options? We might be communicating, somehow—albeit crudely—but few would mistake what we're doing as exercising any genuine language.

And what if I spend an afternoon poring over a Latin or ancient Greek text, or trying my hand at deciphering some ancient hieroglyphs? Nobody pronounces these sorts of "utterances" any more—in fact, we might not even know what the correct sounds are—but that hardly denies the linguistic status of those marks on paper.

And then there is the question of American Sign Language and its other geographical signing counterparts. Are they "real languages" too?

We didn't used to think so. But based upon Bill Stokoe's groundbreaking work in the 1960s, we now have a very different and measured appreciation of what, linguistically, sign languages are all about. Although it hardly happened overnight.

Carol Padden, the Sanford I. Berman Chair in Language and Human Communication at UC San Diego, began working with Stokoe as an enthusiastic sophomore in the 1970s. She vividly remembers the widespread reluctance of both the deaf and hearing communities to embrace Stokoe's ideas.

*"I was there almost at the beginning—1974—it was only about 9 years after Bill had published his dictionary of American Sign Language (ASL), but people thought he was crazy. They thought it was a vanity project and wondered why someone would make a dictionary that had no pictures of signs in it. He had developed a code for the hand shape and the movement because he wanted a phonological, phonetic analysis of how the movements came to mean things.*

*"But deaf and hearing people alike thought it was a fool's project, that he was just doing this because he was a little bit crazy. In reality, he was just his own person: he was an independent thinker."*

It turns out that Stokoe's insights didn't just make us better appreciate ASL, they shed vital light on how to characterize **all** languages:

*"He published A Dictionary of American Sign Language on Linguistic Principles, meaning the idea of dividing a sign into multiple parts, not simply examining how it looks.*

*"The same basic hand shape could give rise to very different signs— using a "C" hand shape, for example, one can sign "drink", "church" and "very smart". They have the same concept of the hand shape, but that's the only commonality. So he looked throughout the language and searched for the distinct relevant parameters to characterize meaning.*

*"Not all characteristics are relevant to meaning. In English, for example, he recognized, that 'th' doesn't have any common meaning. Take the words 'there', 'wither', and 'path'. The 'th' is the same in all three of those, but the function is different. So he found the different parameters throughout the language and analyzed where a sign was produced. For example, a sign can be produced at the chin, as in 'drink', or at the forehead, as in 'very smart'. You move the hand shape to different places, which changes the meaning. What type of movement matters as well. So for 'drink' the hand shape goes up,*

*whereas 'very smart' stays on the forehead. 'Church' goes up and down and has a bounce to it, and so forth.*

"*Bill notated and coded those things and put them into a corpus. He didn't include every sign, because the dictionary wasn't big enough for that, but he included a good subset of the signs. That seemed to be a good idea.*

"*But in 1965, people wondered why he would do something like that. They wondered, What's the point of such a dictionary? Now we understand. The point is that humans build structure: they create words, sentences, clauses, phrases—very complex entities and utterances.*"

Now that we have a deeper understanding of what languages are, complete with an explicit understanding of the linguistic complexity of ASL and other sign languages, we are naturally better equipped to compare and contrast them.

And, equally importantly, we are finally in a much better position to appreciate how they came about in the first place.

A key aspect of the development of any language—signed or spoken—Carol realized, was gesture. But for years, gesture was a veritable third rail for sign language linguists, given their natural concern that many would regard **all** sign languages as just a glorified form of gesture.

"*When I started, we wanted to keep a distance from gesture, because people would say, 'Oh, it's universal. It's the same thing.'*

"*And we would say, 'No, it's not. It's different.' One gesture, like thumbs up, can mean a multitude of different things, including: 'Good job', 'It's working', 'See you later', 'Everything's good', 'I'm fine', 'You can leave', and so forth.*

"*But in sign language, you would have a different sign for each of those expressions. You have a lot more specificity. You have words that you combine and recombine. So we needed that distance from gesture, because a lot of that work was really looking at co-speech gesture, which is what I'm doing right now as I'm speaking: I'm not signing.*

*"Gesture follows the rhythm of speaking. Sometimes you can use it to refer to the size of something, like by saying something is small, or saying that it was roughly this size or that size. Co-speech gesture is very much linked to what you're speaking. There are lots of ways that gesture seems so different from sign language, and we wanted to emphasize that difference.*

*"Thirty years later, I think we've made our point. Now, what I'm doing, together with some of my colleagues, is going back to gesture and thinking about how languages come into being."*

Thus equipped, Carol and her colleagues have carefully investigated the advent of new sign languages throughout the world, from Israel to Mexico to sub-Saharan Africa, carefully documenting their distinct evolutions.

*"You have a community that's closed for some reason—maybe it's geographically distant, maybe it's ethnicity, maybe it's an island—but for some reason they're kept separate from schools, from national sign languages. If you have a mix of deaf and hearing people, they will spontaneously begin to create a new sign language from gesture.*

*"In the first generation, it really starts to take on properties that are distinctly different from co-speech gesture. It's different from pantomime. It's a little bit more than pantomime. Then you have a second generation, in which the language really starts to take shape, and by the third generation, it really starts to look like a lot of other sign languages in the world. So in a span of about 75 to 80 years, you can build a new sign language out of gesture, and it has all the indications that we recognize to be true of sign languages that are much older."*

And while Carol focuses on the development of new sign languages in particular, it's important to stress that these languages are hardly exclusively used by and for the deaf—an often underappreciated fact that speaks volumes for both the linguistic power of sign languages and the intrinsic merits of diversity, points we would all do very well to bear in mind in this increasingly homogeneous world.

> *"The thing about a lot of these communities is that it's not just deaf people who are signing; hearing people are doing it as well. Their siblings, their relatives, their neighbours—a lot of them will say to us, 'Why are you here? You came all this way to see us do this? This is as natural as breathing. We just wanted to communicate.'"*

# The Conversation

# I. Choosing Languages

*Faulty assumptions and different sides*

**HB**: To begin, perhaps we can talk about how we're doing this, and some of the difficulties that you were mentioning earlier about the decisions that have to be made when you sit down to do an interview or talk to somebody—the "political issues", as it were.

**CP**: [Speaking] Right. Every time I go into an interview, or if I'm giving a talk, or if I do something spontaneously, I have to decide which language to use. In some situations, if there are a lot of deaf people, I prefer to use American Sign Language.

So, I would just sign [begins signing] like this and allow Mala, my interpreter, to speak for me. This is the most comfortable thing for me. I don't have to think about how I'm pronouncing a particular word or how I'm going to state certain things because I grew up with American Sign Language, and it's my first language, my home language. I'm very comfortable with it.

[Speaking] But if I'm in a different situation where, maybe, there aren't any deaf people there, then I prefer to just speak English without signing, like I did with you when we first met.

However, this means that I'm not available if deaf people are watching the video or watching the event. I have to weigh, *Do I use the language I'm most comfortable with? But the voice is not me; it's somebody else* with issues like *Well, that's what other people might be more comfortable with, or might work best in that particular situation.* Another issue is that a lot of people have the idea that if you know sign language, then you **must** use it, because you can't speak English.

That's not the case though. So I'd like to switch back and forth so you can hear what I sound like when I'm speaking myself and then hear what I sound like if somebody else is speaking for me.

Mala has worked for me for 12 years, and she knows what words and sentences I like to use, and so forth. So this is the closest thing to me actually speaking, but it has the feeling of a different voice, a different person talking while I'm signing. So I'm just going to switch between these two ways of speaking.

If a topic is perhaps more personal, then I may want to use American Sign Language for that. If we're talking about technical things—like spoken language and sign language—then maybe I'll switch to English.

Sometimes there will be a person using American Sign Language and that person doesn't speak. Sometimes you're fortunate to have a great interpreter like Mala, but sometimes you don't have a very good one.

You may think, *Does this person really sound like that?* You have to remember that the process is one step removed. So I want to illustrate how the same person can sound different, or just slightly a little bit different, depending on what medium she's speaking in.

I grew up using American Sign Language. Both of my parents are signers, I have an older deaf brother and my parents are deaf, so sign language was completely natural to me. I've used it my entire life—so, for me, switching between languages is a natural thing to do. They both feel like they're me, but they're different sides of me. You'll see that when I start signing, I might express myself a little differently than I do when I'm using English.

**HB**: I'd like to probe you a bit more on this idea of different sides of you. I've heard that said by many people who have command of two or more languages. They feel like they are somewhat different people when they speak a different language. But before I do that, and before I go into your personal background, I want to ask a question about what you just said with respect to Mala.

You mentioned how Mala is an excellent interpreter and how you've been working with her for 12 years. When you first started working with her, was there this sense of a connection with her that you might not have with other people? Has she changed very much in those 12 years? Did it take 2 or 3 years before you really felt you were on the same wavelength?

**CP**: Honestly, I can't remember. I began working with Mala because she's one of the best interpreters I know. She's highly qualified and has very good training. I think what happens in the relationship of working with an interpreter, in a job like this, is she understands when I want to sign or use spoken English, when I talk with a person one-on-one or use an interpreter, and so forth. We've become accustomed to being in many different situations, so we know what to do and at what time.

But she's also a linguist by training, so she knows a lot of my vocabulary if I'm signing about something technical. If I have to give a large, keynote talk, I prefer to sign, if I can. I just don't have to think about it. I feel like I can be more spontaneous.

Whereas if I'm speaking English, I feel like I'm more guarded. It feels like I need to think what the next word will be—maybe not subconsciously, but I feel more protective if I'm doing it in English. I feel like I'm a little bit looser, a little bit more spontaneous, if I'm signing.

But Mala just *knows*—she's heard all of my jokes, for example, ten times over. She knows the joke, so she can time it exactly, almost all the time. It's really about that comfort—when you walk into a situation where people really don't know anything about signers, or don't know anything about me, then having the confidence of working with an interpreter I know very well is one less thing to worry about.

**HB**: What happens when you want to come up with a new joke?

**CP**: Maybe you should ask Mala.

**Mala**: I freak out a little bit.

**CP**: Mala likes to be thoroughly prepared. If I have notes, she wants to read them in advance. But sometimes, in situations like this, we don't have notes, so we're flying a little blind here.

**HB** (To Mala): So you are out of your comfort zone now?

**Mala**: A little bit.

# Questions for Discussion:

*1. If you see someone signing do you naturally assume that she can't speak?*

*2. What do you think makes "a great interpreter"? To what extent does it involve more than knowing how the person likes to express herself? Do you think that there's an objective difference between the act of interpreting from a sign language to a spoken language and interpreting from one spoken language to another?*

*3. Do you feel somewhat like a different person when you are speaking another language?*

## II. Distance Education

*A formative experience*

**HB**: You mentioned having deaf parents and a deaf older brother. My understanding is that you didn't go into an English-speaking environment until grade 3 or thereabouts. I'd like you to tell me not only how that experience was for you and the impact that it had on you, but I'd also like to get some general understanding of the circumstances. Why did your parents do that at that particular time? What were their motivations, and were they pleased by the result?

**CP**: My parents are both academics. They're retired now, but they were both on the faculty at Gallaudet University in Washington D.C. They both graduated from there and then they both became professors. My father was an athlete, so he became a professor of physical education, and my mother was a professor of English literature. As a result, I grew up in a home talking about ideas, talking about teaching, talking about university. Now that I'm working in one, it feels like an extension of my childhood.

But my parents' life was very different from mine. They both went to boarding schools for deaf children, which was the norm at the time. My dad graduated from Gallaudet in 1945, my mom in 1947. They both went to schools where they lived year-round and only came home on holidays. They grew up in a segregated environment. Deaf people went to special schools and hearing people went to what were called public schools.

I was born at a time when people were starting to think about inclusion. They didn't call it that then; they were thinking about mainstreaming, but that word hadn't yet appeared. I was born hard of hearing, and I went to a deaf school, an elementary school on the

Gallaudet campus. But when I was in first or second grade, one of the school administrators approached my parents and said, *"Carol is learning English quite well. She's hard of hearing. Have you thought about having her go to public school?"* These days we would say you're being mainstreamed, but at the time, it really meant going without an interpreter, going alone.

In this case, I went to a school with a very small, experimental program with a few other deaf children. It was an hour bus ride from my home—they were bringing deaf children together from a very wide region in Maryland. I remember leaving the familiar environment of my school, on the same campus where my parents taught, to travel for an hour to a public school.

I went from a class of maybe 6 to 8 children to a class of 30 children. It really felt like a huge transition. I went for a year; and then, at the end of that year, they said, *"Carol seems to be doing fine without an interpreter. She can go to her local public school."* For most of my life, until my first year of college, I never had an interpreter. I was the only deaf child in my school. In many ways it felt like being educated abroad: I would go to school, I'd come home and use sign language with my parents and talk about what it was like.

But that experience naturally produced a certain distance between us. My parents grew up in a school with all deaf children, whereas I grew up in a school where I was the only one. So I think my parents felt that distance. I certainly felt it. It felt like some things would be hard to explain, that I had to limit myself, so that's what I've done. I think I'm very acutely aware of what it takes to communicate, how cultures are different, and how to reach people. That's something I've always had to do.

# Questions for Discussion:

*1. How do you think Carol's experience in public school might have been advantageous to her future career development?*

*2. If you had a deaf or hard of hearing child, would you be naturally inclined to "mainstream" him?*

# III. Signing as Language

*Bill Stokoe and the development of ASL*

**HB**: When you were going through this long period of "studying abroad", as you put it, from primary school all the way up through college, were there other people who were reaching out and wanted to learn American Sign Language, wanting to make an effort to get out of their comfort zone to better communicate with you—other students, or teachers? Did you have those sorts of experiences, or was it all about *you* having to adjust to the prevailing environment?

**CP**: A lot changed between third grade and when I began teaching here at UCSD, a lot of ideas about sign language changed. American Sign Language wasn't even officially called American Sign Language at first. My father never had a name for sign language when he was growing up, he just called it "sign language" or "signing", and that's what I called it.

It wasn't until about 1965 that there was the idea that sign languages are different in different parts of the world—people just naturally think it's universal. Bill Stokoe first identified what he called "The American Sign Language" and it became the official name for the language. But *we* just did it. It was simply what we did.

When I was growing up, when I went to public school, I had friends who learned to finger-spell, but not to sign, because that's not what hearing people did. Signing was just for people who don't speak, for those who have no other alternative.

But Bill Stokoe's initial publication made people stop and think, *Wait, we need to take another look at this*. Ideas about language changed and it became a subject of study, which to this day amazes my parents—that so many people out there are interested in what we do, interested in sign language. Sign language used to be thought of as something "for those poor, deaf people", but now there are all these people learning it. Friends of mine who have deaf children who go to public school now find a much more receptive attitude towards sign language.

My daughter is hearing. In passing, she'll say something like, "*Oh yeah, my parents are deaf. I grew up signing*," and people will say, "*Awesome!*"

She experienced a very different reaction than I did—it wasn't something you hid, but it wasn't something you expected people to be interested in, or expected people would want to learn themselves.

**HB**: When, all of a sudden, it went from "signing" to "The American Sign Language," did that change the actual language in any way? Was there a sense of codification or a sense that "***This*** *is now part of American Sign Language and* ***that's*** *not*"? Or was it just a seamless transition from what you were normally doing to something that was just called something more official?

**CP**: It wasn't sudden. It took a period of time. I know this because I was very fortunate: I transferred to Georgetown University as a sophomore. I started out at California State University, Northridge because they had interpreters, and I wanted interpreters because I had never had them. But I also wanted to do linguistics, and Georgetown was the top place for an undergraduate degree, so I transferred to Georgetown after one year.

I also wanted to work with Bill Stokoe, who had a lab at nearby Gallaudet University. I approached him and said, "*I want to work in your lab; this is what I want to do.*" And even though I was just a sophomore, thank goodness he said, "*Sure. I know your parents. I teach in the same department as your mother. You can come and work with me.*"

So I was there almost at the beginning—1974—it was only about 9 years after Bill had published his *Dictionary of American Sign Language*, but people thought he was crazy. They thought it was a vanity project and wondered why someone would make a dictionary that had no pictures of signs in it. He'd developed a code for the hand shape and the movement because he wanted a phonological, phonetic analysis of how the movements came to mean things.

**HB**: Because he was treating it as a real language.

**CP**: He was. But deaf and hearing people alike thought it was a fool's project, that he was just doing this because he was a little bit crazy. In reality, he was just his own person: he was an independent thinker.

I remember, I think it was the first or second year I was at Georgetown—I would go back and forth between Gallaudet and Georgetown so I could work with Bill—I had the idea of having a reception so people could come to our lab and see what we were doing because people were saying things like, "*What are they doing up there on the third floor? They're videotaping, they're working, there are all these graduate students. What's going on?*" So I thought, Why not have a reception?

We picked a day, we ordered the food, we ordered a little wine—he was very classy about that kind of thing—and hardly anybody showed up. We were there with all this wine and food and nobody came.

Now he's revered as one of the most original thinkers in our field: almost any kind of publication that talks about the history of ideas about sign language will cite him.

Many, many years later—this was shortly before he passed away—we had a conference in honour of him and his work. And I turned to him and said, "*You remember the reception we had and nobody came? Well, look at this room now. It's filled with 300 people! All these people are coming to a conference just for you.*"

So things didn't change all of a sudden. It really took a change of ideas, not just about sign language, but about language in general. It was this idea that language has structure and properties, and these ideas are still changing. That's the work that I've been doing for the last decade or so with my colleagues. We've been focused on looking at new sign languages in other parts of the world—not here in the US, but elsewhere.

# Questions for Discussion:

*1. Did you think that ASL was "a real language" before you began reading this book? Do most people?*

*2. Are some academic disciplines more open to new ideas than others?*

# IV. Diversity and Structure

*The many shades of sign languages*

**HB**: Describe to me some aspects of the differences between sign languages. You said a moment ago that it's a popular misconception that there's only one sign language. Tell me about the different sign languages that exist today and some of the relevant aspects of the history. How did that come to pass?

I can imagine that it might have just been a natural process, as with any language—you have dialects and distinctions based upon the fact that groups of people are out of contact with other groups of people and they develop their own ways of communicating. Or is it somehow different than that?

**CP** [Signing]: Maybe this is a good time to use American Sign Language. You'll see for yourself.

American Sign Language is used in the United States and English-speaking parts of Canada, and it is also becoming a major world language in other places where they'll use it for national and regional sign languages.

But many different sign languages exist around the world. We're not exactly sure how many there are. We're starting to find more and more and discover new ones. You can find a comprehensive database of languages at a website called ethnologue.com

There you'll see a myriad of sign languages and they're adding more all the time. They have sign languages in Brazil, Guyana, Japan, China, Korea, and so forth—I'm sure there are different sign languages in the North and South parts of Korea.

But people think it's universal because it's gestural. We think of gesture as universal, so the thinking is that sign language must be too.

But, in actuality, when you have a culture or community of people who are together and share a particular language, distinctions arise.

We're not really sure when American Sign Language dates back to, but people often pinpoint a particular time in history, in 1817, when the first school for the deaf was established. We do have records of sign language communities and users prior to that, all the way back to the 18th or even 17th century. We can't exactly pinpoint the date when American Sign Language began, but schools are often a good indicator because people live in a particular place and all of the children come together and begin to develop a common standard, if you will, a conventionalized sign language or signing behaviour that's developed from that group.

If you go to Europe, for example, you'll have French Sign Language, German Sign Language, Italian Sign Language, and so forth. Each different nation will have its own sign language.

**HB**: So help me out here, because I want to know a little bit more about the linguistic structure. The fact that different regions have different sign languages doesn't actually surprise me, but I'm curious to know if there any structural links between these different languages.

For example, you can look at a language like English and say that it is historically and structurally closer to German than many other languages. Similarly, you might look at some Asian languages and trace them to a shared origin. You might talk about Proto-Indo-European and all that. I'm wondering if maybe there is something similar with sign language as well.

To be more concrete, I'm wondering whether, if you go to France or Brazil, you can understand a little bit of what these people are saying when they're signing? Does it depend on where you go? What are the commonalities?

**CP** [Signing]: Very good question. You have to remember that I've been talking about what Bill Stokoe did in 1965. As I mentioned, he published *A Dictionary of American Sign Language on Linguistic*

*Principles*, meaning the idea of dividing a sign into multiple parts, not simply examining how it looks.

For example, the sign for "drink" seems to be someone holding a glass and bringing it to their mouth. That's an ASL sign for "drink".

Other parts of the world have other quite different signs for "drink". But what Bill wanted to do was try to point out and describe what the hand shape was. So there would be a specific code for this hand shape—"C"— to which you would add the movement behaviour. The same basic hand shape could give rise to very different signs—using a "C" hand shape, for example, one can sign "drink", "church" and "very smart". They have the same concept of the hand shape, but that's the only commonality. So he looked throughout the language and searched for the distinct relevant parameters to characterize meaning.

Not all characteristics are relevant to meaning. In English, for example, he recognized that "th" doesn't have any common meaning. Take the words "there", "wither", and "path." The "th" is the same in all three of those, but the function is different. So he found the different parameters throughout the language and analyzed where a sign was produced.

For example, a sign can be produced at the chin, as in "drink", or at the forehead, as in "very smart". You move the hand shape to different places, which changes the meaning. What type of movement matters as well. So for "drink" the hand shape goes up, whereas "very smart" stays on the forehead. "Church" goes up and down and has a bounce to it, and so forth.

Bill notated and coded those things and put them into a corpus. He didn't include *every* sign, because the dictionary wasn't big enough for that, but he included a good subset of the signs. That seemed to be a good idea.

But in 1965, people wondered why he would do something like that. They wondered, *What's the point of such a dictionary?*

Now we understand. The point is that humans build structure: they create words, sentences, clauses, phrases—very complex entities and utterances. American Sign Language is at least 200 years old although we refer to it as very young.

How long have we been talking and analyzing sign language in this way? I'm guessing about 60 years—not that long. Spoken languages have been debated and analyzed, their historical relationships with other spoken languages examined, for so many more years. History dictates that English has a very long and rich history, and sign language isn't quite there.

We don't yet have a map, so to speak, of how spoken languages are related to sign language. First, we need to figure out what the geography of deaf people is. Where have they lived? When do people sign? Is it only deaf people who sign or do hearing people sign?

All of these questions haven't been asked before: we've never been interested in them, or we didn't need to know the answer before. Now they've become interesting and necessary questions, and we're ready to ask the exact kind of questions that you just did.

## Questions for Discussion:

1. *Why do you think that Carol suspects that there are different sign languages in North and South Korea? What does this imply regarding "political factors" influencing linguistic development?*

2. *How might the act of concentrating on the structure of sign languages have resulted in the development of important general linguistic concepts and approaches that might otherwise have gone unnoticed or unappreciated?*

# V. Distinctiveness

*Language, identity, and the question of affordances*

**HB**: I'd like to know how it feels personally, as opposed to some general theoretical framework—

**CP** [Speaking]: Before you go on, what did it feel like to hear me speaking English and then rapidly switch to signing?

**HB**: What did it feel like? Umm. It was fine.

**CP**: Does it feel disembodied?

**HB**: Well, it feels a little different, because the voice was coming from Mala on my right, instead of from you, I felt the urge to turn and face Mala, but I quickly told myself, "*That's stupid,*" so I didn't do it.

**CP**: That's natural.

**HB**: It felt a little weird, but it's fine. It's actually very interesting.

**CP**: Does it sound like me?

**HB**: Umm...

**CP**: See, that's the thing.

**HB**: Well, I don't know you that well, of course, which is surely a key factor in all of this, but it sounded a bit, the sense that I had was that while signing you had perhaps a bit less hesitation in your responses. Maybe that's just because of what you told me before, but it seemed like you felt that it was, somehow, more natural, that you were a tiny bit more natural signing.

Again, it's quite possible that I'm just projecting what you told me before. I don't know. You seem very natural in English, frankly, and if you hadn't mentioned it earlier I probably wouldn't have said that.

**CP**: I want to convey that I'm essentially the same person, but I'm using two different, what we call "modalities", and that's what's really interesting about sign language work.

If you are using the visual modality, is the language structurally different somehow? Expressively, yes, but is there something different about the language if it's expressed in this medium or expressed in speech?

**HB**: From my perspective, it seems that there are two slightly different issues here: there's what is being conveyed—which involves the analysis of the semantic content and so forth—and then there's the idea of, not only how it makes you feel, but what sorts of things you talk about and what your thinking patterns are.

I'll speak from my personal experience. I've spent a lot of time in France. My French is not as good as my English, but it's not bad. And I feel, when I'm speaking French, a little different. I feel, personally, that I'm a little bit of a different person. I don't want to exaggerate here—I don't feel like I'm an Asian woman, or something like that—but I do feel that I'm somehow a slightly different person, that I have somewhat different thoughts and somewhat different thought patterns.

I've talked to many people who have similar experiences. I think part of that is because the structure of the language somehow imposes certain thought patterns on you. I don't know how to describe it. You're the linguist. But, anecdotally, my own experiences are such that I do have somewhat different thoughts when I'm in that environment, whether it's cultural, linguistic or combinations thereof. I can imagine that it might be the same for you and for other people who are bilingual.

**CP**: Absolutely. This is well documented: languages are world-views. They're a way of configuring the world and a way of thinking about the world. The language you use provides you a vehicle for that relationship with the world. As a result, when you change languages, you change that relationship slightly. And I feel that not just in how I convey ideas.

With sign languages, we can now ask a slightly different question: Are there *affordances*? Are there things that you can do if you're in the visual modality that you *can't* do if you're speaking? Or vice-versa: Are there things you can do when you're speaking that you *can't* do in sign language?

We've had a hard time getting to that question because, at first, we needed to establish—as Bill Stokoe was so motivated to do—that we're not talking about something that's "sort of like" a language; we're talking about something that *is* one.

In the 1970s and 1980s, how did we demonstrate that ASL *is* a language? A lot of the research looked at the grammatical properties of a language. We wanted to show that we had words, we had a phonology—we have something like phonemes, but not exactly like phonemes. For example, you have words like "there", "weather", and "path". The phoneme for "th" is respectively at the beginning, the middle, and the end of those words. It's about the sequencing.

In sign language, we don't quite have the same kind of sequencing arrangement, but we do have it in part. That was the brilliant discovery that Bill made, to talk about what these parts were and how they were arranged. There's *some* sequence, but mostly the parts happen at the same time.

Then we wanted to show that there were sentences, so my PhD thesis was about how we know we have the idea of a subject—the subject of a clause, or a direct or indirect object. How would you make an argument for that in a different modality? That was my whole thesis. I talked about verb agreement and I talked about different types and properties of verbs. That was in 1983.

Now, here we are many decades later, and the world of ideas about language has shifted. When I started, we wanted to keep a distance from gesture, because people would say, "*Oh, it's universal. It's the same thing.*"

And we would say, "*No, it's not. It's different.*" One gesture, like thumbs up, can mean a multitude of different things, including: "Good job", "It's working", "See you later", Everything's good", "I'm fine", "You can leave", and so forth.

But in sign language, you would have a different sign for each of those expressions. You have a lot more specificity—you have words that you combine and recombine. So we needed that distance from gesture, because a lot of that work was really looking at co-speech gesture, which is what I'm doing right now as I'm speaking: I'm not signing.

Gesture follows the rhythm of speaking. Sometimes you can use it to refer to the size of something, like by saying something is small, or saying that it was roughly this size or that size. Co-speech gesture is very much linked to what you're speaking. There are lots of ways that gesture seems so different from sign language, and we wanted to emphasize that difference.

Thirty years later, I think we've made our point. Now, what I'm doing, together with some of my colleagues, is going back to gesture and thinking about how languages come into being.

This is the work my research group has been focused on for the last 12 years. My colleagues and I—Mark Aronoff from Stony Brook University and Irit Meir and Wendy Sandler from the University of Haifa—began working in a Bedouin village in southern Israel to carefully examine this process of new sign language formation. This is a situation that nobody had recognized until recently, but we now realize happens regularly all over the world.

You have a community that's closed for some reason—maybe it's geographically distant, maybe it's ethnicity, maybe it's an island—but for some reason they're kept separate from schools, from national sign languages. If you have a mix of deaf and hearing people, they will spontaneously begin to create a new sign language from gesture.

In the first generation, it really starts to take on properties that are distinctly different from co-speech gesture. It's different from pantomime, it's a little bit more than pantomime. Then you have a second generation, in which the language really starts to take shape, and by the third generation, it really starts to look like a lot of other sign languages in the world. So in a span of about 75 to 80 years, you can build a new sign language out of gesture, and it has all the indications that we recognize to be true of sign languages that are much older.

**HB**: Do you have enough data for this? You talk about these Bedouins. That's one interesting case. Do you have 20 examples? 30 examples? Do you have enough that you can start making generalizations?

**CP**: We do. There's now a community of researchers who have worked in Bali, Ghana, Mali, and several places in Mexico. Last summer, a group of us working with researchers at Tufts University went to a village in Southern Turkey. The community was smaller there, but we saw the same thing. You want to go some place where, by the third, fourth, and fifth generation, you're no longer able to see the beginnings of the sign language in the oldest people, and you can see the latest modifications in the youngest generation.

Now, the thing about a lot of these communities is that it's not just deaf people who are signing—hearing people are doing it as well. Their siblings, their relatives, their neighbours—a lot of them will say to us, "*Why are you here? You came all this way to see us do this? This is as natural as breathing. We just wanted to communicate.*"

What we're seeing is the natural ability to begin building a language any time, anywhere, given a certain set of circumstances. You can't really see that with spoken language, although you can see it with pidgin, where people meet each other and they don't speak the same spoken language, so they come up with something like a Hawaiian pidgin, which is actually quite old. Other examples include Haitian creoles, Jamaican creoles, and Bolivian creoles. A lot of these were languages created out of African languages that were brought by slaves who were brought to these plantations and combined with the European languages that were spoken: French, German, English, Dutch, and so forth.

Together, you get a new creation. It's not Dutch and it's not one of the substrate African languages that was brought there. It's something new. But it started from other languages that already existed.

But with sign languages, you can actually watch gesture coming together and making words and sentences. That's been my project.

# Questions for Discussion:

*1. Do you gesture a lot when you talk? Does it depend on who you are talking with or what you are saying?*

*2. What might be some of the affordances of sign languages—what might you be able to do with a visual language that you can't do with a spoken one? What might be some of the affordances of spoken languages?*

# VI. Embodiment

*Making sense of the world around us through our bodies*

**HB**: I've heard of something called "The Motor Theory of Speech Perception" or "The Motor Theory of Language." (For some related background on this theory, readers are referred to the Ideas Roadshow conversation with Greg Hickok, *Beyond Mirror Neurons*.) Would you say that this concept of how sign languages evolved from gestures into a full-blown, developed language has any tie-in to these ideas?

**CP** [Signing]: That's a great connection to what I'm doing. I'm going to switch back to signing because now I want to talk about that, specifically

The idea about the relationship between motor aspects of the body and language itself, you're right, has been around for a long time, but recently people have begun to think about a similar concept called "embodiment". Embodiment is our way of talking, our way of signing, our way of behaving and interacting, and it comes from how we interact with the world around us.

For example, if you think about an expression like "the foot of the mountains" or "the head of the class", it becomes clear that there are a lot of ways that we use the body, or parts of the body, to make an analogue with something in the world.

In sign language, that's even more natural to do because you can show it with the sign. It seems pretty clear. For example, if I'm signing something like "drink" or "eat", it would naturally involve the mouth, rather than my arm, say.

In sign language, then, you have new ways to think about embodiment. Some people here at UCSD are doing very interesting work on embodiment. Ben Bergen is looking at ideas about exploring the relationship between people thinking, speaking and anticipating how the body will move. Ben and others are trying to think of language as embodied.

**HB**: *All* language?

**CP**: Yes. With spoken language, if you look deeply enough in places that people have never explored before, you can find examples like "the foot of the mountain", "the head of the class", or "on the shoulders of giants"—giving images of the body as you build meaning. With sign language, we draw on that, we often draw on how the body interacts with the world around us.

Here's another example. I've started to work with the ideas related to signs for tools in sign language—they tend to show what you *do* with the tool, examples include signs for "hammer", "toothbrush", "saw", "broom", and "rake".

That seems very natural, but it also seems that the kind of sign where you show the related movement are for things that are man-made. If you're talking about fruits and vegetables, on the other hand, signs tend to change a little bit: they emphasize the shape of the object as well as, sometimes, how humans interact with it. Examples here include "watermelon", "orange", "apple" and "banana".

But with tools, you tend to stress how you hold them, how the body is interfacing with the world. So you have a separation between things that are man-made and things that are from the natural world, not of the body.

With "watermelon", I do show that I'm thumping on it to do something with it, but signs for "toothbrush", "hammer", "saw" and so forth, are clearly more action-based. We've started to analyze those things, and people are beginning to think about resulting classifications for spoken languages as well.

**HB**: As you were talking, you made me think of a neuroscientist I spoke with who does fascinating work with monkeys (i.e. Miguel Nicolelis—see the Ideas Roadshow conversation *Minds and Machines*), but what seems relevant here, I think, is that his thesis is that the human brain is somehow programmed, or has an innate disposition, to "absorb" tools, neurologically-speaking. So, for example, we have this notion of a tennis player whose racket is a part of his arm— well, to some extent that *actually happens* neurologically. This seems connected to this idea of using tools, incorporating tools, and this sense of embodiment, as you're saying.

**CP** [Speaking]: Yes. To come back to what I said before, the question is: does the modality give you certain types of affordances? When it comes to sports, often the sign is the predominant action of that particular sport, like the sign for tennis or basketball.

What we've done is to go around to different cultures and asked both gesturers who don't know signing and signers of different, unrelated sign languages around the world to look at pictures to compare and contrast the results with our own experiences.

Take the sign for mop, for example. In ASL, the sign for mop involves an aspect of pushing, but in a Bedouin culture, you typically don't push a mop, you slide it. On the other hand, we will sometimes slide a mop while they will occasionally push it.

That is to say *embodiment* is not so much a reflection of my personal experience, but rather my cultural iconography of that particular meaning.

That's why sign languages are not universal. You have different bodily experiences around the world, and the expressive potential of the language changes. You have some signs that don't look anything alike, but then you look at them and you think, *Oh, of course!*

My colleague, John Haviland, who is an anthropologist here at UCSD, works with a very new sign language in Mexico that is only one generation deep. He's looking at the very beginning. When we began working with Bedouins, the first generation had already passed away, so we were working with the second and the third.

One of the things that John likes to do is to go up to people and ask them, "*If you were to come up with a gesture for "chicken", what would it be?*" What would you say, Howard?

**HB**: I hate these sorts of tests. Maybe something to do with an egg. I'm not sure.

**CP**: Imagine yourself in a marketplace and you're trying to buy a chicken.

**HB**: See, that's my problem. I never go to markets.

**CP**: All right, fine. You're off the hook here. But a lot of people will, say, flap their arms like wings, or they might waggle their finger like a chicken's beak, or they might smooth their hair back in imitation of a chicken's comb.

But in this family's first generation sign language, the sign for chicken is to rapidly wring its neck, because that's what they do with chickens. That's embodiment.

Why don't we use the same sign? It might have something to do with our taboo for talking about how you prepare food for consumption. This is why sign language is not universal. But it is based on gesture.

My group is looking at the co-immersion of meaning and structure from its roots. People try to communicate and people want to communicate efficiently, so the language has to become faster. How does it become faster? How does it become as fast as American Sign Language?

It's so fast that I'm sure you couldn't recognize the individual signs. Maybe you could pick out one here or there, but on the whole it's very efficient, whereas if you look at gesture, it's not. It's very laborious to do gesture after gesture.

We're very clear about what's different between gesture and sign language. Now we want to think about how you *make* a language. If we can figure out how you make one, then we know exactly what its properties are.

# Questions for Discussion:

*1. How might our language have evolved differently if our bodies were different?*

*2. Carol talks of how cultural iconography affects meaning for gestures—and, consequently impacts the development of emergent sign languages. Might it also be the case that it works the other way around as well, so that gesture affects that surrounding cultural iconography? In other words, to what extent does the way one mops in a particular place, say, get reinforced by the way that gesture is incorporated in the development of the regional sign language?*

# VII. A Cultural Window
*Change, humour and balance*

**HB**: Is American Sign Language changing? Is it evolving? If we were to have this conversation 20 years from now, is there a sense, based upon what's happened before, that ASL will have changed in a way that renders it more efficient or something?

**CP**: Languages don't exist in a vacuum; they exist in real life. Some things become more frequent, other things become much less frequent and they disappear. How long will "whom" continue to be used, do you think? It's getting to a point where it's hyper-correct if you use it. That's just one clear example. Another example is that there are suffixes that we used to use a lot but no longer do. All languages are constantly in a state of evolution, and they're also devolving.

Migration also has an effect on language. For example, people from Southern Sudan flee because of war, so they leave Sudan and they move to other parts of the world and then they lose the ability to speak the language that they spoke in Southern Sudan because they're not there anymore. As a result, the language begins to drop certain features because they're no longer surrounded by other speakers of the language.

War, genocide, sometimes modernity in itself plays a role: sometimes young people stop speaking languages just because they're not hip or cool anymore, so they drop them. Languages die as well as come to life.

**HB**: Have you noticed American Sign Language evolving in your lifetime? Are there phrases or expressions that were prevalent when you were younger that are no longer used now?

**CP**: Absolutely. My parents use a different language than either I do or deaf people younger than me do. The funny thing is, sometimes I meet hearing children of deaf parents who grew up in a family using sign language, but learned English and didn't interact with other deaf people. They go off to college and they're not part of the deaf community. Some of them take classes with me. They come up to me after class and say, "*I don't sign very well, but I have deaf parents and I grew up signing, and I'd like to introduce myself.*" They're 18 years old but they sign like they're **50**. The language is frozen in their parents' generation. It's so remarkable. When I see them signing I'll think, *Oh, my Dad does that!* or *I know older people who do that.*

**HB**: Can you give me an example?

**CP**: It's in the movement. It's a very subtle thing. My other interpreter has deaf parents. We were working somewhere and I saw her do an older sign for "fast". It's just a difference in hand shape, but the first one is older and the second is newer. So I told her, "*You sign like your parents,*" and she said, "*I know, I know.*"

That's the thing I like about working with coders: sometimes it can be a sort of flash from the past. There will be a small thing like the substitution of a hand shape, but you get this feeling of age. It's something that feels rich and deep, just from something small like that.

**HB**: I'd like to talk a little more about the interplay between language and culture. One can talk about the English—that is, the English from England—and their sense of humour. Or you can talk about a style of mathematics, or painting, or whatever, that comes from different places.

I was recently talking to an analytic philosopher in Los Angeles (see the Ideas Roadshow conversation *Appreciating Analytic*

*Philosophy* with Scott Soames). My conviction is that there seems to be a causal tie between the structure of a language—this Anglo-Germanic style of language—and the development of something like analytic philosophy. There's probably a reason why it didn't come from the French, or the Italians, or something like that.

I started thinking about things like senses of humour, plays on words, and puns. There does seem to be a difference in terms of jokes, or humour, or plays on words, that can be done, certainly between English and French. They're both very playful, but they play in somewhat different ways.

What can you say about American Sign Language and the sense of humour, and puns, and the blurring of the language—perhaps poetry as well. Because of your complete fluency in English, of course, you can look at these things and compare.

**CP**: Yes. There's a slightly different style of humour when I'm signing. One of the funniest things you can do is to adopt the mannerisms of a different person signing. It's like changing your voice to mimic someone.

We can do somebody very familiar. We can mimic a very well-known deaf person and people will say, "*I know who you are!*" just like somebody can mimic Robert De Niro or John Wayne or somebody like that. We can do that too.

Jimmy Fallon does this all the time: he has this sulky teenager voice that he does and people know exactly the type of person he's referring to. You can do that in sign language too. You can mimic a hearing person, you can mimic a new signer, you can mimic a very conservative, hard-nosed kind of deaf person, or you can mimic a flaky person. You can do that by just very subtly changing your movement and your body positioning, and you can make people laugh doing that. You can convey sarcasm and all sorts of different things.

I have a very good friend who has this unique way of being funny. She does it out of the blue, and when she does it you can't help but laugh.

When you sign, you have signs like "deaf" or "home" and you sign on one side of the body—typically, if you're right-handed, you sign on the right, while if you're left-handed, you do them on the left side. And what she does is, instead of doing "deaf" on the right side, she does it on the opposite side, which is funny. I know it's not funny to you, but when she does it, I'll be on the floor laughing. But I can't tell you *why* it's funny. It's just so clever, and nobody does it; so when she does it, it's just unique and hilarious.

**HB**: But that's what's interesting, because, of course, jokes often don't travel well from one language to another. That's one of the cruxes of this notion of humour and language and culture. It's exactly that: *I* don't find that funny because I don't understand the entire framework. I don't have any reference to draw on.

**CP**: Right, you have to live the framework too.

I haven't spent a lot of time analyzing what a punch line would be and how a punch line would work, but one of the funniest things for me is to show the reaction of the other person, that sort of blank expression people sometimes have on their face, for example. I can't do it, I can't quite think of it right now—[Carol begins signing]—but if I were signing I probably could.

[Speaking again] Because I'm constantly traveling between different cultures, I really like these things that are crazy-different, because it shows you the wacky possibilities of language.

What happens if telling a joke is slightly different because you have a different apparatus? In sign language, you use your body in a way that you don't use it in spoken language.

People think about language universals, but sometimes that becomes too abstract. Sometimes in order to find something that's sufficiently common across all languages, sign languages and spoken languages, you have to reach a level of abstraction that almost makes it no longer descriptive.

**HB**: Right. It becomes almost sterile.

**CP**: Exactly. You lose the embodiment part of it, which is fascinating. But my colleagues and I think about language as working with what you have, and *only* what you have. Speech has a little bit of gesture; you're not completely devoid of it. People are beginning to realize how multi-modal language is. You could have just recorded this conversation in audio, but you're doing it in video too. Why? Because there are things that happen in video that are not captured in audio or text. You get a richer sense of what's being said.

People understand this now. I think we're beginning to appreciate that what signers and speakers have in common is not necessarily some abstract idea of language universals. Rather, what they have in common is that all humans have the potential for multi-modality. We're all multi-modal, but we choose different configurations of that multi-modality to build a language. That's really what we're working with. We want to see why sign languages end up with this particular configuration and why spoken languages end up with a different one.

There are some spoken languages that often utilize something called an ideophone. There are languages in which you click. There are languages that use sound symbolism. We use a little bit of that in English, but in Japanese, for example, it's used more often. You begin to see all the differences across all languages—that each of them represents a certain subset of the entire possibility of communication in all human beings.

I think of sign languages as being transmitted across time, and generations, and a culture, and a community that's completely infused with the need to communicate. It's this wonderful blend of creativity and structure—structure to allow for a certain degree of conventionalization and creativity to find new forms of describing how the ways of the world are changing.

# Questions for Discussion:

*1. Do you think that English is evolving faster, slower, or at the same rate than at other times in the past?*

*2. To what extent is it possible to "translate" the humorous content of a joke from one language to another? (Readers particularly interested in this notion are referred to Chapter 3 of the Ideas Roadshow conversation* **Babbling Barbarians: How Translators Keep Us Civilized** *with Princeton University translator and bestselling author David Bellos.)*

# VIII. Predictions and Proclivities

*Speculations on the future, fillers and gender markers*

**HB**: From this sense of different modalities and the fact that you can use this notion of embodiment in far more descriptive ways using sign languages that you don't have using a language like English, or presumably most spoken languages, one comes face to face with the notion of the richness and uniqueness of the experiences that are conveyed through language.

That, in turn—or at least it seems to me—brings us to this notion of deaf culture. One can imagine a world—pick a date, say 200 years from now—where people say, "*We have to move towards a time when we can eliminate deafness from the world*." And, as a likely consequence of that, we can imagine that all of these languages—all of these unique ways of communicating ideas, that whole structure—would be eliminated, which would be a horrible diminishment of the richness of the human experience generally, together with our scope of communicating different thoughts and concepts.

You've written quite a bit about that. Years ago you wrote a book called *Inside Deaf Culture* with Tom Humphries. I'd like to talk to you a little bit about that and how some of these related notions might have changed in the interim, both in your mind and in the public consciousness.

**CP** [Signing]: You're right. There could be a day when people don't sign anymore. I doubt it will be in my lifetime, but it could well happen. There are people who think, *Why bother with signing? If you can speak, why bother? Just go ahead and use speech and we all will understand one another.*

If that were true, then war wouldn't occur if everyone spoke the same language—but that's another topic altogether.

I think people don't understand diversity, and they don't understand why we need diversity. Many think something like, *Deafness is a form of suffering. You have to sign. Don't you want to be free of the obligation to need an interpreter, the difficulty you experience communicating, etc.? Why support small languages when you have English? It's a perfectly good language.*

That's an ongoing issue. It's the moral debate that continues for people who study languages.

And languages are dying. I've heard a statistic that said something like one language dies every two weeks—languages we've never heard of. If I gave you a list of languages that have died in the last year, I doubt you'd recognize any of them. There are languages all over the world where, once the last speaker is gone, the language dies with that person.

Sign languages die as well. There are sign languages where the signers have withered down to one or two people and when they pass away that language will be gone. American Sign Language has about 200,000 or 300,000 users, but ASL users are in other parts of the world as well, although we don't document them.

So what is the future? I think it's time for my husband and I to write a new book, actually. There are many new things to say about all of these issues. Some people ask themselves, *Should I get a cochlear implant, because that might lead to the disappearance of sign languages?* People think about what will happen to sign languages if they close schools for deaf children.

But then again, I meet people who have never been to a deaf school: they grew up in public schools, and they don't meet a lot of other deaf people, but they decided that they just wanted to learn to sign. Some of these people are great signers, and they didn't have to go to a deaf school or learn sign as a child. There are hearing people who sign very well—many more people today than in the past. We never thought that we would see so many. The number of signers is perhaps doubled, if you count hearing people. 200,000 to 300,000 people use ASL as a primary language, but if you add people who take ASL in the United States in the colleges and universities around the country, that number is much larger.

I just met someone at a conference who was learning ASL on YouTube. He just decided that he wanted to learn it. He's Korean, and he wanted to learn because a lot of conferences will have ASL interpreters, but they might not have Korean Sign Language inter- preters. So he did some research, went on You Tube, and found some instructional videos. He's pretty good for a person who learned from the Internet—not bad at all, I must say.

People learn English from watching American TV. They learn it in school. So maybe our whole methodology for learning languages is changing. I don't know.

**HB**: Is there a related issue with American Sign Language versus other sign languages as there is to English versus other languages? Do you have people who are proponents of Korean Sign Language or French Sign Language and exclaim, *"These damned Americans are taking over!"*?

**CP** [Signing]: Yes, definitely. Andrew Foster was an African-American missionary and he decided to go to Africa and set up deaf schools. I don't know how many deaf schools, exactly, but he set up many in Africa.

At the time—I believe that was the 1960s and 1970s—he thought that we should encourage using ASL because it's a good language, but at the time people didn't understand the richness and importance of encouraging people to build their own language. As a result, many parts of Africa learn and use ASL.

When I look at African signers, I don't actually understand them. It's a different dialect of ASL. It's hard for me to understand them, but they sign ASL. They said, *"It's great to know ASL because, now, I can go to conferences around the world. My country can't afford a sign language interpreter, so I go to other conferences and the US has money to send their interpreters there. I can watch an ASL interpreter*

*and understand them. I have no problem. I use my sign language at*
*home, but I'm glad I use ASL too."*

So there's that too: the economic value. The richer language is often more accessible. But it doesn't have to be one or the other. You can know more than one language. You can know two, or three, or four; and that's perfectly fine.

**HB**: I don't know what this is called—I'm not a linguist, so you'll have to tell me—but Mala just said, "*You know.*" When one speaks, one says things like "like", or "you know". Do you actually do that sort of thing too when you're signing? Do you use those—whatever they're called—those "pause things" when you're signing?

**CP** [Signing]: Yes, we have explicit signs for "*Wait, there was something...*" and that sort of thing. We call them "fillers". You don't want someone looking away during a silence, so you want to keep the floor, as it were, and people keep looking if you continue to speak. That's the principle of holding the floor.

**HB**: Interesting. I can also imagine, in terms of vocabularies, that with regard to sign languages, there would be one language—maybe it's American Sign Language, because it seems to be very prevalent, popular, and developed—that has a greater or richer vocabulary, or what have you.

Is it the case that one can look objectively at some of these different sign languages and say that some have, at some level, a greater power of expressiveness—by whatever metrics you want to use—just as some people might say that English has a much larger vocabulary? Now, that doesn't mean that you can't say things in other languages, of course...Maybe I should start that question all over again...

**CP**: Yes, it's very risky—it's very risky to go down that line...

***At this point we take a short break and change interpreters.***

**HB**: During the break we were talking about how different people sign in different ways, like "masculine" versus "feminine" signing. The specific example that was used was the sign for "fast", where one way to do it was considered particularly "masculine" and another particularly "feminine". The notion that there would even be such a distinction would never have occurred to me.

**CP**: Sometimes you may hear someone say something and you think, *Oh, that sounds like a very Southern California way of talking* and you envision an image of a particular type of person. So when I think about the signing for "fast," I imagine a type of person who might use one version of the sign "fast" in a way different than another person who might use the other hand shape for the sign "fast".

The use of the whole hand to sign "fast" is a little bit heavier. It seems older, maybe. It's one word, and the pronunciation of the sign kind of gives you an image of the person, or people, or the place that might use that sign. That just happens naturally with languages.

**HB**: But can you generalize and say something like, *"That's a macho or typically testosterone-riddled way of signing"*?

**CP**: Sure, but it's really hard to separate the body from that. A very masculine body would have an effect on how that person uses the space between their arms and their hands, and how they hold their body, the tempo of their movement, and so forth.

An interesting thing about language is that you tend to recognize things that are stigmatized. In speech, you might recognize a ditzy person by the way they say something. There's an expected standard for that kind of person. You recognize something about it. But we all have dialects, different variations of the way we speak. There are ones that are stigmatized and we tend to talk about those more often, or we recognize them more often. We mark them or label them more often, but all of us have variations in some particular way.

# Questions for Discussion:

*1. Do you think that there will be fewer people speaking sign language 50 years from now? More?*

*2. Why do you think Carol says that "It's very risky to go down that line"? What are the risks, exactly? Do you agree?*

*3. Is it reasonable for Howard to be so surprised that there are highly "masculine" and "feminine" forms of sign language expression, given that the same thing exists with voices in spoken language?*

# IX. Examining Diversity

*Brain scans, sign-twisters and gesturing Italians*

**HB**: I'd like to turn now to the question of what's happening in one's brain when one is using a language. A classic example that most people have experienced is, if they find themselves in an immersion experience where they're learning a new language, there's a certain time when they develop a facility and a familiarity with the language, and one threshold is that they begin to dream in this language. Is there something analogous that happens with sign language?

**CP** [Signing]: Sure. Sometimes I dream in sign language. Sometimes I dream that I'm speaking English, or Spanish, or French, or something else. Sometimes I'm signing in dreams and I can't quite seem to express myself—you know that feeling of being stuck in mud and you can't seem to get out of it? I've had all those types of experiences.

**HB**: That makes me think of impediments. Of course there are those who have some form of speech impediment, but there are also just phrases that are difficult to say: tongue twisters and that sort of thing. Are there signs that are just hard to do and others some particular people really struggle with?

**CP**: Yes. There are two different issues. The first is language difficulties like stuttering, language delays, or what is called a specific language impairment. We're finding out more about those in sign languages.

There are deaf children who sign and the teacher and the parents look at them and think, *There's something going on here. There's something about this child's signing that seems impaired in some way.* We didn't have the tools to look at this before, but now people are doing this kind of research. People are describing cases of children who are having a very difficult time using their space while signing.

There was an important publication by David Quinto-Pozos from the University of Texas about a child who had a difficult time with using space, setting up things in space to convey his ideas through sign language. Now, the next step is to try and figure out what kind of difficulty is it exactly and what it says about how the brain works.

The other thing you were talking about is tongue-twisting or sign-twisting, where it's a slip of the hand rather than a slip of the tongue.

There is published work in that area as well. Take the sign, "to cook". Maybe you have the wrong hand shape or you swap out one hand shape for another, because you're thinking of a fork but you want to say "cook" and you use the hand shape for "fork" but you're signing "cook." I'm not sure if that's a good example or not, actually....

**HB**: I had the opportunity to talk to Ellen Bialystok (see the Ideas Roadshow conversation *The Psychology of Bilingualism*), who's a psychologist who studies the effects of bilingualism in the brain. Using techniques like fMRI and MEG she and her colleagues have observed statistical similarities in some features of the brains of bilingual speakers, including—not surprisingly given everything you've been saying—those like yourself whose bilingualism involved a sign language.

I'm guessing that there's probably lots of other work happening now at the crossover of linguistics and neuroscience, doing various fMRI studies of people who use sign language, say. Is that true? Is that a booming field right now?

**CP** [Speaking]: It is. There are a lot of people working with fMRI, with MEG, with ERP, and other studies with signers. It's not work that I do, so I don't feel that I can talk about it at length, but there has been an explosion of work on sign language structure, on small sign languages as well as larger, national sign languages. There is also related work on sign language acquisition in young children.

Before I was talking about language impairments: signing children, both deaf and hearing, who seem to display something that's not quite typical—we now have the ability and the tools to go in and describe exactly what the impairment is and then to be able to link it to particular parts of the brain and ask ourselves which parts of the brain are related to comprehension and production.

Sign language is about the body, but it's also about using the space in front of the body. So you can make a map. If I were describing how to get to some place, how to travel, I would make a map, sketch it out in front of me. You can do that horizontally or vertically. There are different ways of doing it.

So when it comes to mapping it out, the question is, *Where in the brain is that happening?* It's language, but it's also visual-spatial, which is in the right hemisphere, but language is in the left. There are a lot of studies about which aspect of space is tied to language and which aspect of language is generally more visual-spatial. The thing with sign language is it flips in and out.

More generally, I think we're beginning to realize that signers also gesture. I talked previously about co-speech gesture. We also have co-sign gesture. This is some of the work that my colleagues and I are doing. A lot of people think, *Well, if you have sign language, what do you need gesture for?* They think that gesture simply withered up, died, and was replaced by sign language. But we're finding that's not correct: signers gesture as well.

We can show this from studies that we've done with young signing children doing a task where they have to describe or talk about a math problem on a board, for example. This is work that we're doing with Susan Goldin-Meadow, one of the leading scientists in the area of gesture.

She has done this work with hearing children, and we did the exact same experiment with deaf children to show that they were using gesture in the same way that hearing children were.

The modality is different between speech and sign language, but it's about conveying categorical information. Gesture is about conveying something that's more continuous, more analogic. But language is purposefully not analogic. It's more categorical.

Sometimes, if you want to show a particular kind of distance, signers will use gesture to show if something is bigger than or smaller than something else. These are the signs for "big" and "small", but with "small" I'm not really showing you how small, and the same applies to "big". If I wanted to show you how small something is, I might make a gesture that uses space accordingly, the same as if I wanted to show you how big something is.

Again, that's why we think of language use as multi-modal. Languages have rich resources, but you end up using just a subset of that. Like I said, some languages have clicks, some have whistles, some use a lot more gesture—like in the Mediterranean area, for example, as well as in Arabic countries. In southern Europe they use a lot more gesture than in northern Europe.

Much of that is shaped by culture and community. Many of these things people once thought were universal, but now we're beginning to really understand how to describe diversity.

# Questions for Discussion:

*1. In what ways might sign language speakers serve as particularly valuable research subjects to help us get a deeper understanding of the neuroscience of language?*

*2. What do you think Carol means, exactly, when she says that gesture is "more continuous, more analogic" than language, which is "more categorical"?*

*3. Might some people be more "hardwired" for learning and using sign languages than others?*

# X. Making Comparisons

*Efficiency, community and complexity*

**HB**: So there's the cultural aspect of this, which I certainly get—I mean, anybody who has been to Italy knows that there's a lot of gesturing that goes on there, a lot more than goes on in, say, Iceland, I would guess.

But there's something else that I think that you're saying. Correct me if I'm wrong, but it seems to me that you're looking, not just at these modalities, but also at functionalities. If we can say, *"Gesture adds this"* or *"Normal language*—whatever that means—*is that,"* then you can start developing some abstract archetypes, or abstract modalities, in terms of what's being conveyed and what tools you need to convey different sorts of things, be it for emphasis or whatever. Is that, roughly speaking, the way things are going?

**CP** [Speaking]: Yes. I think you tried to ask me earlier, but I may not have gotten to it. You wanted to know if languages varied in efficiency and functionality, and I said that was kind of risky.

There's this idea that all languages are equally complex. There are no languages that are simple and no languages that are more complex. All languages do what they need to do. Some languages have 9 or 10 genders. They tend to be smaller languages, and they're very detailed about categorizing the world.

On the other hand, English has no grammatical gender, but you wouldn't say it was less complex. Some people have said that English is ideal as a world language precisely because it does not have multiple genders and it does not have the complexity of verb agreement that you find in other languages.

Small languages can be quite complex because they're very detailed about naming. They're very detailed about subtypes. They have names for lots of different things that we don't have a name for in English. Once you start trying to develop a metric, the metric is always specific to the purpose.

**HB**: Here's my problem with some of this—and I say this as a complete non-specialist of course. Let me set it up with an anecdote. I was talking to one of your UCSD colleagues who studies language and the use of language: Victor Ferreira (see the Ideas Roadshow conversation *Speaking and Thinking*).

We had a very interesting discussion that began with him explaining some of his research of how people use the word "that" as an indicator. One might think, in normal communication, when I'm speaking to someone that I'm preoccupied with how they might understand what I'm saying, but the truth, according to his research, is that most of the time I'm actually not doing that at all. It seems that, most of the time at least, given everything else that is going on in my brain, what I'm really focusing on is finding a way to efficiently say what I want to say rather than worrying too much about whether my interlocutor will understand it.

In other words, there is this natural focus on the efficiency of conveying information. And naturally associated with that are, I believe, aspects of what you just referred to: the potential or real egalitarianism of languages—they're all just means to an end of conveying a certain thought or idea, sending it from A to B.

My problem is that linguistic communication is not just all about efficiency, at least for me. Just using one language, namely English, I find that often when I slow down, when I use an effortful way of thinking so that I don't just run off at the mouth, but instead take a little time to search for my words and think about the right way to express myself and think about the subtleties involved in language, I do a better job of actually communicating, of expressing my thoughts.

To me, at some level, that's the most significant thing

I realize, of course, that most of the time people are simply talking to each other and there's thus an emphasis to look at things as information being conveyed in the most efficient way possible: "There's a hunter over there, we'd better get out of the way."

But when I'm thinking about using language as a means of transmitting more subtle ideas—when I'm playing with the language, thinking about how best use irony, say, or maybe trying hard to write a great poem so that I can convey an abstract sentiment or veiled meaning, then it seems to me that I'm doing something quite different.

Which is all to say that it's not entirely obvious to me that any language will be best suited to being able to do that, and I might be able to make distinctions. Maybe not. I'm not making distinctions between people. I'm not making cultural distinctions. But at least it's logically possible for me to say, *"This language is a little bit better suited to this particular end than that language, for whatever reason historically or otherwise."*

It might be the case that, for whatever historical reason, there are languages that have a particular richness in a certain area which have the tools to convey some particular ideas in a more efficient way—in a deeper way, say—than another language would.

**CP**: Right. You might say German is better for certain types of philosophy. But what are you going to do? Are you going to go learn German?

**HB**: Well, there's the practical aspect, and then there's an abstract, theoretical point. I'm talking more on the theoretical level here. Could it be that some languages naturally give us the tools to be able to achieve some ends, in a way that can be distinguished from other languages? That's all I'm asking.

**CP**: I think so. That's called diversity. People do recognize that different languages offer different possibilities that other languages don't. Then it's just a practical matter. So even if we could find the best language for something, there's then the very practical problem of how you're going to get access to it, and how you can learn it well enough to actually take full advantage of it.

You might decide that sign language is great for certain types of poetry, but then there's the practical matter of knowing it well enough to be able to create that kind of poetry. Languages are both very easy and very hard.

When I started working with this Bedouin village sign language I spoke about earlier, there were about 3,000 people living there. They don't really have a sense of how many deaf people they have, because who's counting? It turns out that, generally speaking, who's counting are the schools, the bureaucrats, the nation with its census-taking needs. A school principal wants to know the answer so as to know how big to build the school, but the community doesn't care how many there are. So somewhere between 100 and 125 deaf people were living in that village, and I think there were perhaps five times that many who sign the language very well.

I figured that, since this was a relatively new language, that coming to it for the first time, it would be very easy. But it's actually very hard. It's harder than a European sign language.

First, the iconography is different. If I go to Europe, there's this, sort of, Western Europe/US type of iconography. Representations of things that you think about, say, are going to involve the head. But, in Japan, for example, the sign for indecision is at the torso, not the head, because for some people certain types of emotions are in the liver, not in the brain.

So you have to know the iconography of the culture because it affects the gesture, and it affects the sign language. As I mentioned earlier, I was in a place where the motion for mopping was side to side rather than back and forth, so I was looking for certain things that weren't necessarily applicable there. Part of it, then, was the iconography, while part of it is the fact that they never meet strangers. Strangers never use their sign language.

They all know each other. That's the thing about small languages that makes them different from, say, English. I've never met you before, but we're here in a room talking among strangers and we understand each other because we're very clear to name things, we explicitly use complete sentences, we deliberately invoke all of these things that are very referential.

But when you're in a very small community, you don't need to be as referential. You can just point and everyone knows what you're pointing to. You don't need to name.

For example, the sign for Gaza in this particular Bedouin village is effectively "*Palestinian, that way*" (Carol points in a specific direction). On the other hand, the West Bank is something like, "*Palestinian, the other way.*" (Carol points in another direction).

This means that you have to know where you are located at that moment to know whether they're pointing to Gaza or Ramallah. They didn't have names for a lot of the different cities. They just had one sign for a specific characteristic of the people living there and then the direction. So it was geocentric. And most of the time I had no idea where they were pointing to. And even if I did, I wouldn't know what the relevance was, because there was a lot of shared knowledge that I didn't have access to.

I thought, *This is crazy. This language is new, it doesn't have a whole lot of structure, and I can't even get past the first sentence.* Now I'm much better at the language, but it really taught me a lot about big languages and small languages. The small ones have extraordinarily complex grammatical structures.

Linguists have noticed this. You would think that the large languages do, but they're actually relatively simple, because so many people are using them, and as a result they, in a sense, lose their sharp edges so that more people around the world can use them.

**HB:** That's really interesting. I could go on for hours, but I realize that I've kept you for a very long time already, so I should probably wrap things up. Is there anything that you'd like to add? Anything that we haven't touched on or that you feel we should definitely chat about a little bit more?

**CP**: We've covered so much. I don't know how long we've been talking for, but we've definitely covered a lot. It's been an interesting conversation. I'm sure I'll think of something at midnight tonight, but nothing comes to mind right now.

**HB**: Well, I had a wonderful time, Carol. Thank you so much.

**CP**: Thank you.

## Questions for Discussion:

*1. Do you believe that all languages are equally complex?*

*2. Do we do a good enough job encouraging people to learn other languages in our society? Does the widespread use of English diminish English speakers from learning other languages and enriching their cultural understanding?*

*3. Can any thought be conveyed in any language?*

*4. How has this conversation influenced the way you look at sign languages?*

## Continuing the Conversation

Those interested in getting a deeper appreciation of some of Carol's views are referred to her a number of her books, including, *Inside Deaf Culture* and *Interaction of Morphology and Syntax in American Sign Language*.

# Perspectives on Mass Communication

A conversation with Denis McQuail

# Introduction

*A Sense of Perspective*

*Quis custodiet ipsos custodes?*

This famous phrase, attributed to the Roman poet Juvenal from his *Satires*, is literally translated as *Who guards the guards themselves?* but is generally regarded as tantamount to simply asking, *Who's watching the watchers?*

In our modern age, where everyone seems to have a camera pointed at everything at all times, "the watchers" takes on a radically new meaning—as does, necessarily, the potential watcher of the watchers.

"The media" often appears as some sort of distinct presence removed from the rest of society—"an unholy behemoth of corporate interests" for some, "an apologist for bleeding heart socialists" for others. But whatever side of the political spectrum you might find yourself on, and however much you might naturally agree, or disagree, with Fox News or The New York Times or Rupert Murdoch, you would be dead wrong to conclude that media, or communication in general, is some abstract entity that is somehow independent from the rest of society.

Closely examining the media—in particular mass media—necessarily involves a careful, probing look at what our society values. The mass media, then, in a certain sense, is a direct reflection on us.

So maintains Denis McQuail, one of the few people alive who has made a serious and systematic study of not only mass media but communication theory in general.

His series of pioneering monographs: *Communication Models* (with Sven Windahl) and *Mass Communication Theory and Media*

*Performance* went an enormous distance towards establishing the entire discipline of communication studies, thereby shedding light on the enormous sociological influence of the media, while simultaneously delineating a clear and rigorous means by which this influence might be measured.

> *"I think that a major flaw in quite a lot of past approaches towards studying media and communication effects was that it was detached from a prior study of society, it was detached from fundamental knowledge of processes of human communication—considering the human context and considering the very great diversity of communication in all aspects of human lives. This was missed, basically.*
>
> *We have to look at how communication is taking place without reference to the technologies—and that applies to the new media and the so-called "social media" as much as anywhere else."*

But what of journalism? What is the link between journalism and our societal values?

Once again, Denis is the perfect person to ask.

Back in the 1970s he was seconded to serve on the UK's Royal Commission on the Press, an event that stimulated him to develop many of the concepts, metrics and ideas that he was to harness so convincingly in his later work on mass media:

> *"We were to make a study of so-called 'standards of press performance', which involved developing concepts that included diversity and objectivity and sensationalism and things of that kind that could be applied to make judgements about British newspapers. The purpose of the thing was to respond to many criticisms of the British press, in particular."*

Some 40 years later, he is still ruminating deeply on the role of journalism and society, still motivated to ensure that these vital issues remain firmly in the public consciousness.

To that end, he recently published a thoughtful and penetrating analysis for journalism undergraduate students entitled *Journalism and Society*.

> *"I thought that journalism students at the first or second year level might benefit from a wider perspective than just the craft or task of journalism—the practical things that they have to learn anyway. It's important to be aware of the wider perspective of their role in society."*

But, as Denis takes great pains to mention, this notion of the wider perspective of journalists' role in society, and our consequent ability to measure and assess it, naturally goes well beyond the interests of just journalism students. It is something that we all have a stake in.

> *"This latest book was fed by preoccupations that I've had for a long time, in particular the development of valuative concepts that could be empirically applied and tested.*
>
> *"So one could make statements about the media or media systems, of particular press organs or broadcasting associations or whatever media services one chooses in a wide range of terms: information quality, communicative possibility, diversity, balance and bias, as well as the independence and freedom that is available to journalists—in theory anyway—and how this is being used, whether or not it has any impact on performance."*

And what of freedom of the press?

> *"Some of the norms of journalistic freedom have been strengthened, but on the other hand, what the empirical research—not so much mine, but from what I can gather of other comparative studies of journalists—has demonstrated strong evidence of a public grassroots resistance to 'too much freedom', as it were.*
>
> *"It's based on a notion of patriotism or nationalism sometimes, a wish for order, and a critique of the excesses of the press. In short, instead of—as one might suppose—principally the powers that be who want to limit the activities of the press, that's not so much the case. There*

*is a strong constituency that sees a completely unhindered press as somehow a societal threat."*

How can that be? Primarily because the vast majority of people in most places don't fully appreciate what the role of the press could and should be.

*"There isn't a widespread understanding of that critical role of journalism or the significance of it. Even journalists themselves are not fully agreed on this. They divide significantly here according to the priority they attach to critical perspectives on whatever it may be—various sources of economic and political power.*

*"And it isn't just journalists, but also the positioning of the mainstream press as an institution in society with a certain sense of obligation, with all kinds of links to clients and contacts..."*

And once again the key point:

*"It's part of the society. The press is not a separate body. It can be identified. It has particular tasks, but it's also very much integrated. And it's also the case that the established press doesn't necessarily see all that much economic self-interest in the activity that some kinds of criticism are."*

Vital questions. And vital reflections. Like the Socratic gadfly, Denis McQuail keeps watching the watchers.

Which is to say, all of us.

# The Conversation

# I. Plunging into the Media

*The beginnings of a unique career*

**HB**: I would like to start by discussing your personal history and how you got involved in media and communications studies, how you moved into this field, and even what the field is, but we'll get to that later. You started off studying history, didn't you?

**DM**: Yes, I did. I studied history and I became rather dissatisfied with it. I also couldn't find the employment I wanted after I was done studying it. In the last year of my studies I had discovered, by chance, something called sociology and that was something I hadn't been aware of at all until that moment. I examined the University of Oxford course calendar and found that there was really only one way to study some sociology in a post-graduate diploma, so I took that.

I developed a very strong interest in social research and surveys, which were possibilities that seemed absent in history, possibilities for coming to some generalizations. History was very particularistic, especially in Oxford. There was a strong resistance to any general conclusions or theories about the world of the past, or even, I suppose, the present. It was very English, or British, untheoretical, empirical study, but empirical in a kind of unsystematic way, whereas sociology promised enlightenment about the world on a much larger scale.

**HB**: So this was more out of the spirit of general principles?

**DM**: It was focused on the possibilities for social research of some kind. I had an idea of doing research in a more applied field, for instance housing and planning. That was one area in which I had an interest, but it so happened that, just by chance, I was offered the possibility of working on a new research unit that was just being set up in Leeds University. This was a project for the study of the impact of television on British society, a topic that I hadn't really thought about before that moment. So I was not seeking to do that, although I had always been interested in film.

**HB**: This was in the '60s?

**DM**: This was in the late '50s. The world of television was only just coming into being in Britain, because television at that time was only just reaching the majority of the population. The project was funded by Granada Television, one of the first of the ITV companies when they started commercial television in Britain. So this study partly had a public relations, good works origin. The owner of Granada Television was socialist as well as being very rich, and he had ideas about doing good in society.

The project spoke to strongly felt anxieties, at least in the cultural elites, about the potential benefit or harm of this powerful new medium, which was only just starting to replace radio as the main entertainment medium. It was a very interesting opportunity and it involved applying the skills of data collection, experimentation, surveys, and analysis, all of which appealed to me very much.

**HB**: Did you find yourself a little bit over your head all of a sudden?

**DM**: Not really. Well, I was inexperienced and young, but I was the assistant to a man who had a lot of experience studying audiences for BBC educational programming. His passion was also the measurement of results and the means by which you can make the best use of a public medium like broadcasting to improve general standards of education and knowledge in the society. So it had a social purpose and it involved quite a lot of experience and knowledge about what factors in broadcasting were most likely to be effective in attracting, keeping interest, and also communicating essential points, by way of different media: print, radio, and then audio-visual means.

At that time, in the 1950s, there was a major preoccupation with how media, different media, would perform in relation to each other. Of course, that has earlier origins in the United States and also in wartime research into propaganda, including motivational propaganda for military recruits and the civilian population. So there was a big impetus behind it. At that time, in the late '50s, in Britain, there was a strong anti-commercial television lobby fearing the results of Americanization, and trivialization, and advertising, and consumerism, and all these things, versus the more high-minded BBC mission.

**HB**: What were the results of this study?

**DM**: Well, the first study was more or less given to us as a requirement. That was the study of an election. In the same year that unit began, when I joined it, there was going to be a general election in the UK. It was the first television election in the sense that it was the first time the majority of the population had television and it was also the first time a lot of rules and limitations on political broadcasting had been removed. Prior to that, television was more or less kept away from the political process. So there were very interesting questions about how this would change the nature of politics and how politics was conducted.

**HB**: And did it?

**DM**: Well, it did change the way politics was conducted a little bit, because a lot of effort and expectation was put into the parties' political broadcasts, which were all broadcast at the same moment: the peak viewing time in the middle of an evening. So they had very large audiences and that was a new factor. It appeared to be a more important means through which people heard about things going on with the election; however, the results were pretty clear that the only really demonstrable, empirical result of television's part in the process of communicating the election, was a general increase in the level of political information. So the medium informed, but it didn't change voting intentions in any systematic way. It could be said that it did not persuade.

The model for the work was studies done in the United States—

**HB**: Well, there was this whole thing with Nixon and Kennedy and the first televised debate.

**DM**: This was just before all that actually.

**HB**: Right. That's what I was going to say, because that's the story that I've heard as a non-expert. You hear about how television affected that election because of the sweat on Nixon's lip and so forth. People developed a visceral dislike for the man having seen him for the first time. And I think he himself said, "*Were it only radio, I would have won this election.*"

**DM**: Yes, that was part of the fear of an intervention of an irrelevant kind in the political process in the UK. As a result of which, no debates were allowed. In fact, not even now is there a proper framework for any kind of leader debate in the UK, as far as I know.

Every party had power at one time or another, and no party, no government, would yield any change in legal regulations that might conceivably give some advantage to their opponents. So it was stalemate. The main concern on the part of politics was that television should, preferably, have no impact at all. No harm in having a bit of information, but better not to intervene in any other way, by way of personalities or what have you.

This kind of result was not unique. Quite a lot of research was oriented towards demonstrating the power of television, which was one of those expectations that generally came with the different mass media since the 1920s, from film and radio, and so on. The outcomes were nearly always no significant differences. Whatever research design or experimental method one applied, as long it was well done, no big change could be found, nothing in public communication.

Now, there were clearly experimental situations for other communication purposes, like education, where differences could be and were found. But, in the public arena, there were basically too many other influences in the world and that led to a general decline in interest in the effects of the media, for the time being anyway.

**HB**: How did that affect you personally? If there was a withdrawal of interest, what happened on a personal level for you?

**DM**: Well, it was a more immediate effect in that my immediate mentor and boss died, unfortunately, when we were just starting our main project on the longer-term effects on the cultural life of the people of Britain. The project was put on hold.

I was left to find intermediate projects, which I did. I wrote a thesis on television drama, again following this idea that television could intervene in the very strongly class-structured pattern of popular taste because it was bringing, by way of drama on both BBC and ITV Commercial Television, quite a lot of plays from the classical repertoire, and newly written plays by up-and-coming authors about contemporary life. A number of people considered this a breakthrough for cultural enhancement and saw it as a change in the distribution of interest in what might be considered better culture or higher culture.

**HB**: Were people disenchanted at some point relatively soon afterwards when they started to see that perhaps television was by no means exclusively used in this particular way?

**DM**: Well, what my research tended to show was that plays of any kind tended to fit into a pattern of expectation for certain kinds of satisfaction. So if people wanted to be entertained, they might be entertained by a Shakespeare comedy without quite realizing that it was supposed to be a work of genius, that it was supposed to be studied intensively. The cultural quality, so to speak, as determined by the relevant elites and experts, was really not relevant to the great majority of television viewers who were watching a play for different reasons, sometimes to learn about life and be interested in the world around them, sometimes for excitement or thrills, or sometimes for general diversion. The key to the pattern of taste, demand, satisfaction, and applause by the audience, was some rather continuous and stable pattern of expectations that varied according to dispositions, life positions, age, and the usual range of human differentiating factors.

Again, it was a mistake to think that you could change fundamental tendencies through an intervention, which, in the end, turned out to be rather temporary because this sphere of high-quality drama didn't last because it was taken over by alternative means of production, and imports, and competition between channels, and so forth.

In the beginning, these plays were actually staged in the studio and just recorded. They were not live, but they were continuous recordings of an actual play being performed in a studio. I saw some of these events. It seems quite strange now. It was even strange then because films were not made like that. Anyway, that was how it was done.

**HB**: There seem to be so many different things that one can study as a sociologist. One can look at cultural issues. One can look at the impact of this new technology on thoughts and minds, on government policy, on politics, on political issues, on sociological issues, and so forth. Was it sometimes difficult for you to take your own particular predilections and biases out of the conversation? Did you ever think, *Well, I'm not really sure I should be studying this phenomenon or that phenomenon because I have passionate views about this myself, in terms of what direction I think society should go,* or does that, in fact, enhance things? Is it the case that you can say, *"I really want to study this because I care deeply and passionately about this particular result"*?

**DM**: It wasn't the latter. It was opportunity and attraction of the moment. After a couple of years of relative anomie in a leaderless department, I was joined by a colleague, a political scientist, who came from outside. We started to work together on new kinds of political communication research, which proved very fruitful and I enjoyed working with the man. I actually went to his 90th birthday not too long ago. He's still going and I find him good company.

Anyway, I liked doing that and I kept doing similar things on and off, but I moved on to other things, because one of the things about the life of a researcher is that there was no career in it. You had to have a proper job, as it were, so I had to get a job as a lecturer.

## Questions for Discussion:

*1. To what extent did television play a different societal role in the 1970s to the one it plays today? Will television still exist 50 years from now?*

*2. Do you think that it's easier, harder, or just as difficult to start new fields of academic research today than it was 50 years ago?*

# II. Getting Rigorous

*"Mass Communication Theory" arrives*

**HB**: Tell me about the evolution of your research—the ideas and the responses to them.

**DM**: The first alternative direction of research that I pursued was this notion of audience motivations. A study of the next general election, which I made with this new colleague, was focused very much on the development of a scheme for, first of all, establishing motives for watching politics on television, or reading about it, or following politics, and then building that into some kind of instrument which would relate the possible outcomes of election and communication exposure to differential motives.

This could be a difference between the motive to have one's opinions reinforced, or the motive to find some new guidance, or it might be the motive of excitement of following the election race, which has always been a strong performer in this scheme. That study actually proved to be actually more fruitful than our earlier research. We came up with some interesting results that explained some differences in the outcome between different parties.

Anyway, we then made studies of a variety of programs, in terms of people's motivation, including soap operas, quiz programs, and so forth. However, I'd became a sociology lecturer and I needed to add some other strings to my bow, as it were, and I got interested in media policy, which was something that fit the profile of the department I was working in, more than audience interests.

**HB**: It seems like this was a natural progression. After all, you seem to be consistently consumed with passion about the public's access to information, how they use information, what that can actually achieve, whether technology can affect it in a positive way, in a negative way, or in any particular way whatsoever.

At some level media is just the tool to provide that sort of access. The real issue is how this affects the hearts and minds of individuals in terms of how they're going to act, how they may vote, what they're going to do, how they react towards each other and so forth. Your overall concerns are on a societal level; media is just the mechanism with which you explore that. Is that a fair statement?

**DM**: Yes, that is true. I think that was a major flaw in quite a lot of the approaches to studying media and communication effects: it was detached from a prior study of society. It was detached from fundamental knowledge of processes of human communication. It was beyond the range of different branches on knowledge which had been explored in the 1950s and earlier, and yet, put aside. There was a kind of immediate payback, in worldly terms, in going to the question of, in practice, what difference it makes to advertisers, or propagandists, or educators. The path by way considering the human context, the very great diversity of all aspects of communication in particular lives, was basically missed.

It slowly became a corrective to some of the expectations of effects. So it became fairly clear that much communication was mediated through personal contacts. Even mass media themselves, although they seemed to be directly received by many people at the same time, are, in fact, received in contexts of family circles or friend circles. They are discussed. They enter into conversation. They are filtered through all kinds of barriers in the social circles of particular groups in society.

Even today, it remains the case that we have to look at how communication is taking place without reference to the technologies; and that applies to new media and social media, as much as anything else. They are generally looked at in isolation from the social relations that really underlie the use of such technologies. Partly that's because that's what the industry wants. That is what the development of the technology requires: that they can make claims for social consequences without reference to any fundamental concern, or knowledge of precisely where they fit into people's lives.

In that period, I spent a little time in the United States, at the Annenberg School for Communication. I became preoccupied with the possibility of pushing forward the idea of a sort of communication science. It was a hopeless idea really, but when I came back, in the early '70s, I did write a book about communication as a social process, in which "Mass Communication" was just one chapter of twelve. It looked at organizational communication, and interpersonal communication, and so on.

**HB**: Why was it a hopeless case? Was it wildly unnecessary, or too ambitious, or what?

**DM**: Well, no one really wanted it. There was no home for it. Universities and academies are organized along departmental lines. First of all, no one had ever agreed on what communication was. They couldn't define it. There had been quite a lot of debate and argument earlier, going back to the '30s, about what communication was. No one had come up with an answer. There was always a big debate, essentially, between those who saw it as transmission of facts, information, and data, like in systems—

**HB**: Like in engineering: data packet transfer, and so forth.

**DM**: Yes, it was like that. It came from the world of the telephone, and telephony, and the scientific basis of that.

On the other hand, there was the perspective that communication is when people come together and become more like each other, which involves kind of a process of osmosis.

**HB**: It also has to do with content at some level. This seems to be a missing ingredient. I'm listening to this and I'm thinking, *We can communicate all sorts of things. We can have a cat communicating "meow" to another cat.*

**DM**: Exactly. When you get to a level of any kind of detail, the territory disperses into fields which are hard to base on any single social-scientific perspective. You've got possibilities from psychology. You've got possibilities from sociology. But "communicology" never really appealed.

The divide over what communication is, is still kind of a ghost in the history of communication and media studies with continued tension between the empiricists, who just want to know the facts, and the outcomes, and the mechanisms by which things happen in a predictable way; and those who were content to observe, understand, and interpret the subjective experiences of those who are involved in these different communication processes. If you like, it's a quantitative versus qualitative divide.

To some extent, it has to do with the mindsets of those who choose to study these topics. And there's an element of fashion in it. At a certain point, in the '70s especially, the more interpretative school gained ground and the field became connected with cultural studies and the study of literature, which was seeking a more secure base than it had in the modern world.

**HB**: So there are these larger issues. But, on the other hand, concrete progress was made; and, it seems to me, much of that progress was made directly through your efforts. When you developed the idea of mass communication in your book *Mass Communication Theory*, that, I imagine, was a watershed in terms of focusing people on a set of theoretical concepts and practical applications of a particular body of work. That must have gone someway by and of itself to define a research area. Is that correct?

**DM**: I think that's true. I mean, it wasn't just me. There were other contemporary and even earlier works which were providing this framework, building it, and making it clearer. But at some point, it cut off, at least in its ramifications. It was still based on the concept of communication as people talking to others. In the end, it was still kind of a transmission process. It was society communicating with its citizens or members. That was an underlying, though not necessarily explicit, element in this framework.

In a sense that corresponded with the reality. If you took, not human communication in general, but public communication and the means of public communication, which always tended to come back to that, then that was the guiding principle; whereas that was not, in many cases, an ideal situation or a wanted situation.

That's another aspect of this field and the way it has developed: there were always strong normative elements in the framing of questions and issues. At the beginning, the strongest normative issue— leaving aside just pure expediency of trying to be more effective as a persuader—was a negative view of mass society and the result of these means of multiple, one-way communication systems, which tended to produce mass behaviour and were reckoned by some to be responsible for certain movements, authoritarian and so forth.

**HB**: Was there any discontent amongst members of the ruling classes? Did they say, *"Who's this fellow McQuail with his theories about how we're manipulating people?"* Did you get any blowback from the authorities?

**DM**: I kept my head down. I was just a scribe who was reporting that there were these dangerous characters with these views that were possibly a little bit unwanted.

The first negative formulation of mass media as a dangerous phenomenon in society was actually a rather conservative one. It saw the media as destructive of cultural life as controlled by churches, religious groups, family, established institutions, and so forth. In a way, it was a fear of a mob or a mass.

That conservative reaction was later replaced, especially after the Second World War, by the influence of the Frankfurt School and neo-Marxist ideas. Several prominent scholars associated with the Frankfurt School, who were émigrés from Germany in the 1930s, promoted a mostly critical view of mass media as a tool of capitalism and oppression. They were influential though, and they caught the imagination of not just young people. They were widely plausible, and still are, as far as I'm concerned.

**HB**: Okay. But I want to know about the impact of, and responses to, your work.

**DM**: I wasn't trying to be an activist. I wasn't trying to influence in any particular direction. I was trying to report what was, to my mind, the truth. It was that kind of attempt to be a critical scholar. I was not trying to advance a particular critical view of the institutions of society, although that must inevitably follow.

**HB**: But there's also the effect, as we talked about earlier, of influencing the discipline itself. There's the meta-effect of how the discipline evolves, how the discipline gains more respect, how it attracts other people into the field.

Of course, at some level, if one is doing applied sociology, if one is trying to investigate and recognize the different effects that shape society's thinking, then one inevitably has to be affiliated with society; otherwise it's just some abstract, purely theoretically removed endeavour that a bunch of eggheads in a university are pursuing.

**DM**: Well, you're right. One is definitely dealing with issues that go to the heart of the power structure and the exercise of power in modern societies.

It's a challenge to anyone who's trying to make sense of different views. Of course, some of the interventions in the field have been more concerned with the political impact and effect, and that's a perfectly legitimate objective. But it's not quite the same as what a social theorist should be doing.

I think there should be a difference between the interpretation of the world and the attempt to change it. When the attempt to change it begins to influence the interpretation, when it's given priority, then it may reduce the theoretical value of what is claimed or asserted. You at least have to face this problem.

My tendency was to sympathize with the critical view, but not to pursue it to a point where, for one thing, it was losing touch with reality and was not going to be very effective. That was not what I chose as my role and I wasn't expected to do that. Some people do that, and that can be done. The study of media and communication is very much a critical inquiry. But that's true of other branches of sociology and social sciences.

**HB**: Well, that's part of the definition of the field. It's a fairly large tent. Some people have their cappuccino with chocolate, some with cinnamon. Different people do different things.

**DM**: That's quite right.

Another paradigm started to appear at a certain point, especially in the late '60s and early '70s. It was linked to the changing media and to the influence of critical theory, and it had to do with the decay or decline of mass media.

The notion that the mass media were in decline was already being voiced right at the beginning of the '70s. There was a good basis for that claim—partly technological. The possibilities for individuals or groups, who were not part of the system, to communicate at will to the public, were multiplying. You had private radio, private television, photocopy machines, cassettes, cassette radios, even the telephone, although, at that time, no one had really thought about what that could do. Nevertheless, it was there.

All kinds of individual and organizable means of communication could be assembled and employed by groups not belonging to the system, not controlled by the system. Up to that point, nearly all mass media had been by way of the established newspapers or the established broadcasting authorities, very much under the control of government.

**HB**: But there were glimmers of other things.

**DM**: Certainly. There were much more than glimmers. There were strongly expressed claims for grassroots communication as an alternative. You had community television, closed-circuit television.

Several of these technological developments opened up a new theoretical framework, a new paradigm, of liberation through communication, not control and massification. There were alternative paradigms for framing theory and framing expectations.

The more liberationist paradigm did not, in itself, depend on technology; but it was, nevertheless, only realizable through technology. It was also linked to developments in the third world and movements on the part of third world countries to free themselves from their rigid systems of news and entertainment distribution, which were mostly controlled by the West—America and Europe—or the Soviet Union.

The old mass communication framework of centralized influence from the institutional power centres—if not government, then similar, related bodies—was being challenged.

**HB**: And, of course, it's been challenged ever more since then.

**DM**: Yes, increasingly. Once the internet and the World Wide Web arrived, many researchers turned to the question of how that would change the context in which, previously, everything had been dominated by centrally provided, distant sources. There were very new, optimistic, and positive expectations about what could happen now.

**HB**: But you can look at this as a continuity, rather than a discontinuity where, all of the sudden, the late '90s happens and people can say, "*Well, we have the internet. We have all these new ways of being able to communicate that are somehow opposed or, at least, can be positioned against the mass media.*" One could say, "*Hang on. Actually, there were opportunities from the 1970s onwards.*"

**DM**: Yes, you could say that. But those older technologies were not on the same scale. These new technologies had become a new kind of mass media. I find it difficult to know whether these things should be called mass media. They were not "mass" in the same sense that the centralized printing and broadcasting media were; but they were "mass" in the sense of being very widely available and open to use to anyone, and so on.

In that sense, they were a new kind of mass media, but a mass media without a purpose. They were marked by diversity, independence, and many other characteristics. They came with no guarantees. They were somewhat random.

But you're right; it was a gradual change. There was no sudden new dawn.

The critique of the old, centralized mass media had been established as a fairly plausible understanding of the world, despite that early evidence of apparently no effects. That was put to one side because it didn't seem to record the reality of experience. It didn't seem that there were no effects. It seemed that there were often quite big effects from these types of media.

Anyway, one concrete consequence of going to the Netherlands was that I no longer spoke the language that people spoke, and they weren't ready to speak English. I tried to learn Dutch.

**HB**: Did you lecture in Dutch?

**DM**: I tried lecturing in Dutch at a later stage. But then the students asked, "*Would you kindly speak in English?*" However, in the end I did end up speaking Dutch.

But it wasn't so much the language as it was the culture. I had lost a feel for the place I was living in. That was what made it hard to do the kind of work that I had done with survey material, focus groups, interviews, and so on. I lost a sense of the place and the history of where I was. I lived there for 20 years but I still couldn't really read the culture of the place. I learned facts. I read books. But you need much more than that to get grips with it.

**HB**: Well, there are all these subtleties that one seems to notice as well: a sense of humour, for example, or the way that language is being played with, and the different ideas that are being conveyed.

**DM**: Well, as I said, there was a feeling of not knowing about where I was or having any feel for where I was. The language was a problem because, in English, for example, I had a good sense of expressions that I could use colloquially, in interview situations, doing surveys, or just talking to people; I could never learn Dutch in a way that would enable me to do that. When those sorts of expressions or phrases are translated directly, they don't work. They don't produce the same nuances of meaning. And to that extent, I withdrew from the type of research that had to be conducted in a direct, personal way.

One intervening event that happened before I left England was that I was seconded to the Royal Commission on the Press to make a study of standards of press performance. This involved developing concepts like diversity, objectivity, sensationalism, and things of that kind, which could be applied to make judgments about British newspapers. The purpose of the thing was to respond to many criticisms of the British press. It was just about the British press.

For a year I worked on developing the concepts and applying them in content analysis. It was theoretical and empirical and it produced a volume of findings that the commission used for some purpose, which had no consequence. But I think it was quite valuable to do it. It was theoretical and practical. I quite enjoyed doing it. I hope it had some beneficial outcome, but it's hard to see whether it did or not.

Anyway, when I was in the Netherlands I found that there was quite an interest in doing this kind of work as well, and in making their television services more accountable by having verbal and conceptual tools for evaluating content and performance.

# Questions for Discussion:

*1. How is the use of communications technology influenced by the political structure and governing political interests of a country or region? To what extent can advances in communications technology influence changes in the surrounding political system?*

*2. To what extent did Denis' communications research heighten his sensitivity to the strengths and weaknesses of living in another culture with another language?*

# III. Journalism and Society

*Looking more broadly*

**HB**: This brings me rather abruptly to *Journalism and Society*, which is a book that came out quite recently. Although, of course, not only are these issues that you have been ruminating over long periods of time, but the evolution of the book started off in one manifestation years earlier. Tell me about the genesis of *Journalism and Society*.

**DM**: I had a contact and friend at the University of Yekaterinburg in Russia. I had done a couple of things for him, including writing things for a little magazine that he had for his students. He asked me to write a small text on theories of journalism. This was a few years ago. So I did that, partly drawing on things I had written already. I put together a summary perspective on theories of journalism for students who were perhaps unfamiliar with the ideas.

**HB**: So this was written for undergraduate students?

**DM**: Yes. This was for the Russian students of journalism in this university. They had no wider publishing plans and I hadn't thought of it as a publishing venture. I already had my own strong interests in journalism but, to that point, I had not expressed that very much, except for the work that I did for the Royal Commission on the Press. I very much enjoyed enlarging that and bringing together perspectives on different aspects of the position of journalism, in terms of key issues to do with freedom, and accountability, and relationship to power.

**HB**: These are issues that resonate very strongly with a wide variety of people. You don't have to be an undergraduate of journalism to appreciate them.

**DM**: No, you don't. But I thought undergraduate journalism students could benefit from a wider perspective than just learning about the craft or the task of journalism, those practical things that they have to learn anyway. So it was a larger perspective on what they were doing in terms of their role in society which I think is a pretty important one.

**HB**: Another interesting dynamic that you focus on is not only the societal role of journalists—what journalists contribute to society and how they contribute to society—but almost the other way around: how society impinges on journalism, and the give and take between these two structures, and how society structures journalists and how journalists, in fact, themselves, structure society. You get political power that comes into play. You have the role of propaganda. You have freedom of the press. You have liberty. You have truth, and so forth.

These are questions that I think deserve a much wider airing and a much wider readership. Did other people respond to this as well? Is the level of readership something that surprised you? Were you encouraged by that?

**DM**: Generally, it has been welcomed in the educational environment. What the wider consequences or reaction will be, I have no feedback at all on. It has only been a year since it was published. I didn't expect it to make an impact because, although I was bringing things together in a way that was not done in other places, it wasn't, in itself, very innovative.

But it was fed by preoccupations that I had for a very long time.

**HB**: Tell me more about some of those preoccupations.

**DM**: Well, I mentioned the development of evaluative concepts that could be empirically applied and tested so one could make statements about the quality of the media, or media systems of particular press organs, or broadcasting associations, or whatever, in a wide range of terms: informational quality terms, communicative possibility terms, diversity terms, balance and bias, and also in terms of the independence and freedom that is available to journalists, in theory anyway, specifically how this is being used and whether it does actually make any impact on how the performance goes, because media vary greatly in how far they're willing to use their independence. They're often inhibited and pressured.

**HB**: As someone who's been looking at the press critically and rigorously from the Royal Commission in the 1970s all the way through to the present, it seems that you are uniquely positioned to have measured thoughts on these fundamental issues on a societal level, as well as the evolution of the press and how things have changed. This commission was in the '70s, so, from an American perspective, this roughly coincided with the Watergate hearings. This is something that, for me at least, was a landmark in terms of the role of the critical press. Now you have journalists who were raised on the lore of *All the President's Men*, Carl Bernstein and Bob Woodward.

Now, you've seen this evolve to the present day situation where the world of journalism has been widely transformed. You have a much greater concentration of power, in terms of who owns the various media outlets. You have what many would consider a critical dumbing down of media to the extent that there is a vast diminishment of investigative journalism. There is not an opportunity for the media to serve their critical, societal function, in terms of being able to inform the body politic and inform the citizens.

Yet, at the same time, you have new technology that allows many people to contribute towards what are broadly construed to be journalistic practices: using their iPhones to photograph tanks that are moving from one place to another, and so forth.

It seems as though we've witnessed a real transformation in the role, the utility, and the manipulation of journalism in our society. But that's my perspective as somebody who doesn't really pretend to understand these things. Is that something that you would concur with? Or are things basically the same; it just looks somewhat different?

**DM**: There are a lot of differences between countries and regions and media systems. It's a bit hard to generalize. Some of the things you said I certainly think are quite true and valid. On the other hand, I'm not quite sure that the United Kingdom—which wasn't a great performer in the '70s—is significantly worse now. The focus in the '70s, from the position of a thing like the Royal Commission on the Press, was not on the liberating role of the press.

Essentially, there were two key things: objectivity, that is to say, people thought it would be possible to have informative, reliable journalism based on facts, which is a somewhat doubtful expectation; and the other thing was that it should not be monopolized by any particular political party. At that time, there was already a high degree of monopoly, and there still is. The monopolists have changed to some extent. Different monopolists have been in charge, although Murdoch just about spans the 30 years, I think.

But the situation in Eastern Europe was quite fundamentally different, because in the '90s they did have a genuine release from monolithic control and there was a flowering of free and independent publications. That remains partly true of Central and Eastern Europe. However, the Russian case is a regression, after, in the last 10 years, having made considerable progress from the Soviet days.

In various countries around the world you have very different situations. But one thing you've got is a stronger sense of a global, journalistic profession that shares aspirations and problems. That is a strength and some of the norms of journalistic freedom have been strengthened.

On the other hand, what the empirical research shows—not so much mine as what I can gather from other studies, especially comparative studies of journalists—is that there is strong evidence of public, grassroots resistance to too much freedom, as it were.

**HB**: Really? How so?

**DM**: Well, it's based on a notion of maybe patriotism at times, nationalism in some cases: a wish for order and a critique of the excesses of the press. And that can move into the area of opinions that are disruptive of order or threatening. So the climate of fear around terrorism, for example, contributes, in part, to a fear of too much freedom. The press should have limits.

**HB**: So there's a wilful self-censorship to some extent.

**DM**: Well, there is self-censorship. But there is, in varying degrees, popular support for this view. It's not only the powers that be that want to limit the activities of the press. There is a strong constituency that sees this as necessary, and this is true of the United States as far as the evidence goes, perhaps more so than other places.

**HB**: But couldn't it be argued that this is a vicious circle, to some extent? Couldn't it be argued that one of the reasons for this collective desire to suppress some information in order to fulfill security needs, patriotic needs, or what have you, is itself a product of the fact that so many people are not sufficiently well-informed, not only of the facts on the ground, but also at the meta-level in terms of the role of journalism?

I mean, if you don't have enough investigative journalists, if you don't have a society that is pervaded by a spirit of critical inquiry, then the members of the society themselves don't fully appreciate the value of that; and then they will be reticent to allow, or tolerate, or perhaps even encourage measures that would limit press freedom. Wouldn't that follow to some extent?

**DM**: I think you're right and that's also very probably the case: there isn't a widespread understanding of that critical role of journalism, or the significance of it.

Even journalists are not fully agreed on this. They divide significantly in regard to the priority they attach to critical perspectives on various sources of economic and political power, or whatever it may be. It's not just through self-interest. It's to do with some sense of—actually, I'm not quite sure, so I'm not going to pursue that.

It isn't just journalists. To some extent it's the positioning of the mainstream press as an institution in society with a certain sense of obligation, with all kinds of links to clients and contacts. It's part of the society. The press is not a separate body. It can be identified. It has particular tasks. But it's also very much integrated with interests, and persons, and personalities, and family and personal contact. Unlimited freedom and exercising criticism on too much of a basis is not what they see their role as. Many don't. Some do and some don't.

It's also the case that the established press doesn't see all that much profit in this kind of activity.

**HB**: You mean financial profit?

**DM**: Yes, the economic self-interest of advertisers. And the audience might get tired of this sort of campaigning, and they may not really want it. They want various forms of diversion, entertainment, human interest, and so on. There's a whole structure of demand and expectation in which the desire for critical perspectives on society and more information about what's going wrong has a limited market. That tends to make the critical role, except in extreme situations—

**HB**: Well, it certainly diminishes the critical role.

**DM**: Well, it diminishes it, but it's also a mixed role. Part of the reason for a public opinion that wants some degree of control of media and the press is based on criticism of what they do: sensational reporting and various forms of bad behaviour that they do undoubtedly get up to.

I think one has to recognize that the press and the media are not, in themselves, particularly virtuous. They're not seen as such and it's not widely understood that a certain amount of license has to go with the benefits of freedom, free expression, and free opinion. The two things get mixed up: a desire for punishment of perceived wrongdoing and also control.

## Questions for Discussion:

*1. To what extent is it possible to objectively evaluate the "quality of the media"?*

*2. In what way does the very existence of government surveillance technology increase the tendency towards self-censorship? For related insights on this issue, the reader is referred to Chapter 4 of **Quest For Freedom** with Queen Mary University of London intellectual historian and political philosopher Quentin Skinner.*

# IV. Bringing It Home
*The view from the street*

**HB**: This conversation is fascinating but, to some extent, frustrating for me. Let me describe my frustration to you. I feel that I have the opportunity to be sitting across from an eminent sociologist who has thought very deeply about these issues, who is tacking rigorously between these two poles that you yourself described earlier: describing the situation, giving a lay of the land, getting a perspective and an understanding of how these dynamics are acting in a very objective, non-personal and rigorous analysis; and at the same time, there's the Denis who has his opinions, who would, I'm sure, in a private conversation, like to be speculating upon what might happen in a better world, or a worse world, or where the frustrations are. I would like to talk a little bit more with the second Denis, who can give me a sense of whether the media, in his opinion, based upon a wide variety of professional experience, is doing its job and how it might be doing that job a little bit better.

For me, as a man on the street, that's what I really care about. Take the example that I gave before about the decline of investigative journalism, or the fact that journalists seem to be sensationalistic, or the fact that so many stories seem to be boiled down to incredibly trivial sound bites, or the fact that I don't get a balanced perspective, or the fact that there are pedants who go on television shows who are self-proclaimed experts, in whom I have no confidence whatsoever, no confidence that they actually have any deep, objective understanding of the situation. As a man on the street, this frustrates me.

Now, I am not a professor of media studies. I am not someone who is involved in the world of journalism. But I have a few obvious questions that I would like to pose to someone who has that experience:

has it always been like this? Am I misremembering things? Is it going in the right direction or the wrong direction? Are there ways that we, as a society, can somehow improve so that we can make the media fulfill what we consider to be its primary, societal function?

Or am I completely misguided? Is it the case that none of that is happening and, in fact, everything is going wonderfully and I'm the one who should take a reality pill?

**DM**: Your first suggestion, not only is there truth in it, but I think the fact that it has always been thus is pretty much on the ball. I don't go back all that far but if I try to think about what the media were like and I knew them to be like when I followed the news pretty closely as a reader and member of the public, in the 1950s and earlier, then things were not as good.

I mean, the war coverage in the UK was very much a propaganda effort, as it was everywhere, and that practice of controlled information flow was respected by the media on the whole—press, radio and, later, television. Television and radio were ultimately subject to oversight by interested politicians and other authorities, and they didn't even want to overstep the mark. They certainly didn't go in for much. They went for minor, investigative activities—I'm talking mainly about the BBC here. ITV had a bit more freedom and produced a few more investigative results. But it was still ultimately dominated by motives of maintenance of order, income, keeping the business turning over, and appealing to customers and audiences.

But I wouldn't like to set myself up as an evaluator of the quality of the media. I think it's clearly not performing very well. Vast areas of it are failing in many respects and, as I said, I think they always have been.

The question is, what to do about it? One of the other strands of my thinking and research has been in the area of policy. For a long time, I have always been interested in what can be done that will realistically make a difference. If you apply the criteria of realistic expectation about the implementation of any mechanism of betterment, or monitoring, or surveillance of what's going on, or quality control, very little seems possible.

But you need to have a notion of how to do that which is consistent, if that's what one wants. If one wants better media, one cannot impose that by diktat, because that would deny the whole basis of freedom of opinion and freedom of the press.

There was another book I wrote called *Media Accountability and Freedom of Publication*. In that book I tried to face up to the contradiction of media freedom, certainly in the form of journalist freedom, which is really nonexistent, because journalists are not really free. They don't have the right of expression that you or I have because they're working for organizations that are accountable for what these employees do, and these employees do what they have to do. That's their job. They have a certain area of freedom, but basically they don't choose what they say or what opinions they have, because that's the editor's job.

**HB**: Can we change that somehow?

**DM**: No, I don't think you can except by diverse provision. There can be different media, and that was the promise of new media: that they would open things up. That's still not impossible, but that has not really been fulfilled. In small ways, it's not absent. There are alternative sources: little channels and blogs and so on, which, if only they had an audience, would make a very big difference. I'm leaving aside the question of who is reached by this possibility and who, in practice, has access, because everyone has got theoretical access; but, in practice, life doesn't make that access available.

The question is, how? This has come up in relation to the recent controversies about the press in the UK and the problem of what to do about the Press Complaints Commission, which failed to do anything about serious complaints. But how do you reconcile freedom and accountability? The book that I mentioned was basically oriented towards trying to solve that problem. I can't say I did, but I reached the conclusion that you cannot achieve the result you want, in this direction of reform, by punitive means, punishment, criminalization, or illegalization of certain types of activity.

It can only be done on a voluntary basis by a form of account-ability which should be part of ordinary, human communication. We should be answerable for what we say and do in public and be transparent about it.

Well, there's no way of imposing such methods—

**HB**: But can we encourage this in some way?

**DM**: Yes, you can encourage it. I think it does appeal to journalists. It appeals to some editors. It doesn't appeal, of course, to the highly controlled management freaks. It doesn't necessarily interfere with the economic purposes of journalism and the news business. But one should develop an expectation that those who are offending against the different norms that have been mentioned should speak up. It can happen through professional development of journalist associations. That's not a complete fantasy.

**HB**: Earlier we discussed this two-way street, as it were: this dialectic between the journalist and society and society and the journalist, to some extent, and these constraints. For the most part, we've talked about how journalists should serve, how they might be encouraged to serve, that we can't punish them into doing a better job. But there's also the sign of whether journalists—and by "journalists" I don't mean the individual journalists; I mean the entire structure—can be sensitive to, either the actual will of the people and the societal needs that exist, or the potential societal needs that exist.

Let me be very concrete. If I'm living in a place where I find that I'm just not getting the right sort of information; I'm getting propa-ganda here; I'm getting propaganda there; but I'm really not getting that sort of information. It's not intuitively obvious that, if I were a well-meaning member of the journalistic establishment, I would have access to that level of frustration, because it's not as if you can measure that very easily; I'm not buying this publication as opposed to that publication. Maybe I'm fed up with all of them. Maybe I don't watch television news anymore because I think it's rubbish. Maybe I'm not participating in all of these blogs because I think these are all just people who are screaming from the rooftops.

Is there a better way for the journalistic industry to be sensitive to societal needs that are latent or that actually exist right now, that can tap into this frustration? I don't think I'm the only person who's frustrated by the fact that I'm not super impressed by what's coming to me in terms of journalism. It's not that I think all journalists are stupid or that there are corporate conspiracies, or presidential conspiracies, or anything like that. But, at the end of the day, when I go to a newsstand, or turn on my computer, or whatever, I don't have a sense that I have access, notwithstanding the technical opportunities, to the quality, diversity, and breadth, of high-level, informative sources that I would like, and that the journalistic community itself would probably like to have.

**DM**: Well, that is not surprising to hear. Part of the point is, *Is one being deprived in a systematic way—is it just kind of random, or is it structured by the needs of the business?* I know, from experience, that that is the case. A lot of it is that. One has to make some allowances for the circumstances under which this project is being put together.

The best one can look for, in terms of structures, is an openness and diversity of alternatives. Any tendencies towards monopolization within the same business framework, or structure, or type of financing, is inimical to the outcome of an informed citizenry.

**HB**: So, what do we do about that?

**DM**: One plank of policy that remains at least somewhat above the fray is anti-monopoly and anti-concentration laws. These are legitimate within the framework of capitalist society. That is an acceptable intervention, whereas giving subsidies to different publications to voice somewhat deviant, new views, or alternative views, is not, although it does still happen a little here and there.

**HB**: And what about state media? We haven't talked explicitly about that.

**DM**: I haven't because I think they too are very different from each other. I learnt that in Holland. There—it's certainly changed since then, but not completely—the arrangement for making sure that there were diverse views was to divide up the whole production and management, and, in effect, the whole ownership—not financial ownership—of different broadcasting organizations between different groups who were constituted, in theory, by associations of members who paid a subscription. This was public television with a central, facilitating organization that provided the news. Now, the news tended to be pretty much like BBC news, but it did have obligations to have different points of view.

Well, that was quite a different system from the British one and quite different from some other continental varieties and actual practices. The state is positioned in slightly different ways in relation to public media. Alright, fundamentally there's a tension between state-sanctioned forms of financing, or controlled forms of financing, and performance by broadcasters.

**HB**: Are there places that do it better than others? Can you point to certain countries or regions where the balance seems to be a little better?

**DM**: I couldn't because I don't have up-to-date information. At one point I might have said that the Dutch system is a very good system, but the fact is that it wouldn't work anywhere else. The BBC doesn't have a chance of working in the United States. Maybe for good reasons, maybe for bad, I don't think it could work.

**HB**: Because of cultural reasons, the wishes of society, corporate structures?

**DM**: You name it. It has no friends basically, except a few oddballs. For instance, even calling it "state media" is a designation that the

BBC wouldn't accept, and I wouldn't either really, because it's not a state broadcaster in the sense of some. There's not much of a future for public broadcasting. It won't necessarily disappear but it's got its own struggles about financing and how it copes with the digitalization and the online world, where it doesn't have a real mandate. It has to fight very strong interests working against it all across Europe.

# Questions for Discussion:

*1. How has the increased concentration of media ownership impacted both society and the media itself?*

*2. Is the recent concern about "fake news" itself a media creation and thus "fake news"? To what extent is the question of the reliability of the media different today than it was in previous times?*

# V. Towards the Future

*Optimism and pessimism*

**HB**: Turning towards the future, I want to take a page out of your book and say it's important to diagnose the issue, and it's important to do that objectively and rigorously. But it's equally important to think about public policy. We need to be thinking about what the situation is, what the lay of the land is, and what we can actually do about it. You've highlighted significantly, and in my view quite rightly, all sorts of different sociological and cultural factors.

However, I think most people, whether they think things are apocalyptic or just sub-optimal, are of the view that, as far as the media goes, we could be doing a better job. The question is, what do we do about that? There's a limited future for public broadcasting. We are now living in an age of different technological tools. We have different models. You mentioned anti-monopoly legislation as one concrete thing that we should certainly be vigilant about. Are there other things that we could, or should, be doing to make the situation, broadly defined, more coherent, more productive, more informative, so that the body politic can actually play a more significant role in what's going on, compared to what it might ordinarily do?

**DM**: Well, I think the general point is that one has to look at the level of structure and try not to focus too much on particular failings and faults, which are subject to disagreements and are impossible to actually validate, although they might be very convincing indeed. You need to make your own judgments, because I think for a society to make that sort of normative judgment is risky, and it's not going to be effective.

I think one needs to consider, as I said, diversity of structure and alternative means. We've had different forms of transmission: we've had the printing press centralized and distributed physically; then we had broadcasting, and an advance on that is, more or less, unlimited airtime availability; then there's the internet, which is, in theory, sources on demand; and now we have the new developments of social media, which claim to provide an extra level of networking for the public, members of society, and communities.

But my provisional assessment is that we are getting a new form of monopoly. What were once very large media organizations, like Google or Facebook, are acquiring great power in the whole market with ramifications that affect the traditional press and broadcasting. It's being done in the name of freedom, diversity, choice, and endless possibilities, but its actual purpose is to maximize the income that can be gained, usually from secondary advertising.

It's a denial of the promise of the internet—I say promise, but of course no one actually promised it. But there was certainly an expectation and a potential that has been lost, or wasted, or not fully realized. There's no motive for the big players to pursue it. They're not really interested in that.

**HB**: But isn't that the central point? If you just leave it up to the profit motive and you don't have any "oversight"—and I say "oversight" in inverted commas because I'm not really even talking structurally—at some level, at some semantic level, you don't have any oversight in terms of the people's right to know or in terms of the content. It's not content dependent at all. It's not about informing people so they can make better decisions. It has nothing to do with that.

All Google is about, for example, and it seems like a reasonable supposition, is making money. They're a corporation and, as such, they want to make money. How do they make money? They make money through advertising and the more people who are watching, and utilizing their services, and so forth, the more money they make. This is something that is, not necessarily opposed to, but certainly orthogonal to the values that we were talking about earlier in terms of the media.

**DM**: Yes, that's quite true. During the very early stages of the development of the internet, there was a new concept of a mass medium that would be based on the personal choice and preference of the individual, known as *The Daily Me*, which Negroponte promoted in the early '90s. I went to see a talk by him in which he produced an early prototype of a *Daily Me* tablet, which a person could use to find the news they wanted, on any topic they chose. So, if you were interested in critical journalism, you could get a daily dose of the topics that you wanted. This could be provided to order.

However, the latest thinking—and I'm dependent here on a book by Joseph Turow called *The Daily You*—the reality is that the information obtained from the harvesting of personal data is used to structure potential markets based on economic classifications which pigeonhole potential audiences into a certain category for a certain kind of content. It's motivated basically by selling goods or advertising. This is part of the so-called big data analysis. All the big players in the internet business are collecting as much data about their customers as possible. The point being that it is not liberating when the providers are actually constructing for you a kind of identity or personality for their own agenda, on the basis of data.

*The Daily Me* doesn't exist because it's not a viable product.

**HB**: Right, because it goes against the actual structures that are in place.

**DM**: That's right. Now, I'm suggesting that you can intervene to stop this. You can't make this illegal. But there must be alternatives to it. It doesn't have to be provided by some benevolent authority, but there have to be some limits set, and the only way of setting limits is, unfortunately or not, anti-monopoly legislation.

Once you have an awareness of what's going on, at least you can begin to—

**HB**: And that's my point. No one is talking about legislating, but a first step, which I think is critical, and which you are annunciating right now, is understanding the situation. I mean, the very fact that you're saying, "*Look, this was the Holy Grail, or these were the envisioned possibilities of the Daily Me 20 years ago. We didn't get there, and this is why we didn't get there: because the corporate structures, the economic structures, the incentives, are such that they will naturally lead us in a different direction,*" that alone, I think, is deserving of being highlighted because that enables us to address the situation.

From my perspective, there are two things: there is that which is fundamental and pre-eminent; but there is also this idea that, even if we were to somehow circumvent this very deep, structural obstacle, so that I could imagine a purveyor and aggregator that was actually acting in my best interest, as opposed to Google's best interest or someone else's best interest, I am not convinced that enough quality stuff is actually out there to be aggregated to begin with, and the reason is that the structural incentives are not there to produce that sort of material. So, from my perspective, it seems there are really two levels.

But I take your point. Raising awareness of this, making people aware of the fact that this was the potential that this sort of market-place of ideas—the freedom, the international aspect, the ability to be able to pick and choose, which exists theoretically—presented 20 years ago, has not been realized. My sense is that not enough people recognize that, not enough people recognize the underlying mechanisms behind it. You still hear people say, "*With the internet, we can all choose. We can all do our own thing. It's wonderful!*" But I don't think they fully appreciate the fact that these systemic, structural effects are in place and are naturally prohibiting them from doing that. Is that your sense as well?

**DM**: Yes, I think that's correct. The effects are not necessarily "natural'; they are man-made, as it were. But they are built in to the main structures that are developing the technology and choosing which applications to use and which to develop on a large scale. The logic of it is known. It's clear that the consequences are therefore predictable, up to a certain point.

One factor that might be overlooked in this preoccupation with the new is the strength of the old. The established press is declining 10% a year, or something like that, in the United States and the numbers are probably about the same in the UK. The fall in the revenue and the audience of newspapers is across the board. But that doesn't necessarily mean that they will disappear. There are still big differences in newspaper reading all over the world.

The other thing is that broadcasting, what we called television, is still there. I saw recently that, across Europe, something like three-and-a-half hours a day, on average, are spent watching television—television in the old-fashioned sense of the term. Ninety-one percent of viewing takes this form in Europe. This means that there is a lot of life left in the existing structures which have not been undermined yet by the alternative providers. There are still means by which these organizations are guided and directed. Most of the established media are institutionally guided to varying degrees. Even newspapers which seem to offend against social norms are nominally part of some systems of self-regulation. So the means by which society expresses some demands and exerts some influence on the quality of the press are still present to a large degree.

That's not very reassuring but it's happening slowly. It's too early to give up.

**HB**: Are you optimistic? That certainly doesn't sound like a resoundingly optimistic statement to me.

**DM**: I'm not terribly optimistic. I'm optimistic, if the world is still in working order, which is a big "if". The human spirit is quite resilient. I'm quite optimistic about the human race, up to a point.

**HB**: Well, that's likely to be the most positive way to end things that we could possibly manage under the circumstances. Thank you very much, Denis. It's been a great pleasure talking to you.

**DM**: Thanks very much for your questions.

## Questions for Discussion:

*1. Is the internet living up to its promise? To what extent is today's media objectively different than it was 20–30 years ago?*

*2. How has social media impacted how people define what is "news"?*

*3. What do you think "the media" will look like 30 years from now? Will "mass communication" be stronger or weaker than it is today?*

# Continuing the Conversation

Readers interested in a more detailed appreciation of Denis' work are referred to *McQuail's Mass Communication Theory* and *McQuail's Media and Mass Communication Theory* (with Mark Deuze).

Many Ideas Roadshow conversations explore various aspects of the role of media in contemporary society, from communicating science (*The Power of Principles: Physics Revealed* with Nima Arkani-Hamed, *Applied Psychology: Thinking Critically* with Stephen Kosslyn), to politics (*Pants on Fire: On Lying in Politics* with Martin Jay, *How Social Science Creates the World* with Mark Bevir), to history (*Turning the Mirror: A View From the East* with Pankaj Mishra, *The Two Cultures, Revisited* with Stefan Collini).

# The Value of Voice

**A conversation with Nick Couldry**

# Introduction

*Looking into the Mirror*

Nick Couldry began his academic career by reading classics and philosophy at Oxford. Then he became a lawyer. And now he is Professor of Media, Communications and Social Theory at the London School of Economics. Along the way he has written about a very wide range of subjects, including ethics, globalization, democracy, technology, public engagement, agency, rituals and many more.

How is it possible that one career trajectory can touch on all these diverse areas?

Well, when you look closely, it turns out that there's a clear arc that links them all together. In fact, as Nick amply demonstrated throughout our discussion, it could be argued that a proper understanding of media, communications and social theory might just require an equal measure of historical appreciation, philosophical dexterity and legal and ethical awareness.

It's important to appreciate where we come from and what we've done. But it's equally important to understand what, precisely, we've been doing along the way, and what we're continuing to do. In other words, it is essential to get a sense of who "we'" are in the first place.

But why look at media at all?

*"I have no particular interest in media texts. I'm not a film buff particularly—not in a way that's relevant to the work I do. I'm not obsessed with television soap operas. I don't love radio or newspapers to the exclusion of everything else. What I am interested in is the idea that we can represent the social through texts and forms*

*that carry a certain weight—so they almost **become** the social for us. And that 'trick', if you like, strikes me as very, very interesting, because it naturally draws you into anthropology, sociology and other areas—effectively, the theory of how societies work at all.*

*"The core question of all my work is, How do we do social ontology? How do we think about the things that are the social, in a society where they have to pass through a process called 'mediation', which is an abstract way of talking about all the things we call media?"*

For Nick, then, media serves the role of a clinical filter, if you will—a way of putting society under a microscope to get the clearest possible sense of what our values are, how we act and why. Rather than an end in itself, we might regard it as an extremely useful tool to examine power structures, political movements, economic interests, democracy and our evolving notion of culture. It is, in fact, one of our principal windows on that thing we call society.

*"I became captivated by this phenomenon that we call 'the mediation of society'. What difference does it make to the thing we think we know as 'society', or 'government' or any of the big abstractions we talk about in the social sciences, when our starting point has to be that these processes work through very complex institutions of mediation—which have their own interests and involve very strong power plays—what difference does it make to something like a society that it is 'mediated' now?"*

And then there's this key point: one essential, yet invariably broadly overlooked way in which a mediated society subtly differs from a theoretically envisioned non-mediated one, is by, of course, the very unquestioned existence of media institutions themselves.

*"As I started to think about what my angle for thinking about media institutions would be—not the text, but the institutions that we call 'the media', if you like—I realized that this was something much less certain and much less studied: How was the legitimacy of media institutions itself sustained?*

*"Until recently, the assumption was that you certainly had a TV and watched a lot of it. You had radio, you read newspapers and so on. And you were broadly oriented towards whatever was on the media wall.*

*"I never really started from that assumption, because I was always intrigued by the possibility that you might turn your back to the wall. You might swivel round and pay no interest to the media whatsoever.*

*"It turns out that media institutions actually have to work very hard to produce the situation where they are the automatic port of call when we want to find out 'what's going on', as we say, 'what's real' in society.*

*"It was this that made me realize that one could use anthropology and sociology to understand those hidden processes, which the media never wants to talk about, precisely because it wants them to be taken for granted."*

And suddenly the mysterious links that run through Nick Couldry's career become considerably more transparent.

If one is driven to develop a legitimately deeper grasp of the workings of society—what it has been, what it now is and what it might be—then what better way to move forwards than by paying very close attention not only to what it consumes and how, but how it regularly values those particular institutions and organizations of consumption—how, precisely, they shape our economic, political, cultural and social interests?

Looked at in this light, then, it is not terribly surprising that Nick Couldry wrote an entire book on Neoliberalism and its effect on the diminishment of Voice. Again, at first glance, this might seem somewhat incongruous: what is a professor of media studies doing commenting on a particular political movement?

But for Nick, it's all of a piece. From his vantage point, what the neoliberals were most guilty of wasn't a set of particular policies and their implementation, but rather their broader meta-policies:

the deliberate diminishment of contrary views and opinions that are the lifeblood of any robust, democratic society.

And far worse still, they often achieved these ends in active collusion with the very media institutions that are naively imagined to be singularly devoted to upholding that very principle in the first place.

Once again, however much he might agree or (in this case) disagree with the particular message in play, that is not Nick Couldry's primary concern.

What he is fixated on is how that message is being framed, and by whom, and how this framing might, in turn, implicate a wide spectrum of other vital functions of what we call society: how we govern ourselves, what cultural values we subscribe to, our ethical and moral framework, the collected image we hold of ourselves, and so forth.

Voltaire once pithily remarked, *"I do not agree with what you have to say, but I'll defend to the death your right to say it."*

But who will defend us if what we say is not heard in the first place?

Nick Couldry is trying very hard to figure that out. And, if necessary, he is more than willing to jump into the fray himself.

# The Conversation

# I. Round the Houses

*From Classics to Media Studies*

**HB**: I want to start by asking you how you began. I know you started off in Classics and then you moved into Law. What is your story, as it were?

**NC**: Clearly I'm a maverick. I've been all over the map. My first degree was Classics and Philosophy at Oxford. I took the typical working-class scholarship route into Oxford using the classical languages. I got in. I became interested in philosophy. Ideally, I would have continued with philosophy, but I didn't have the confidence at that stage, for various reasons, to remain an academic.

**HB**: What part of philosophy interested you the most?

**NC**: I was quite interested in the philosophy of language, but also ethics. Because I was doing Greek, we studied Aristotle and Plato in the Greek. I could have done that, but there was a decline in the employment possibilities for philosophers in the 1980s in Britain. So maybe I'd made the right move.

**HB**: Well, philosophy of language and ethics, I suspect, have continued to inform your work. It's not as if you've gone completely away from that.

**NC**: You're right. We will definitely come back to ethics, which I've found myself drawing on more and more. But at that time, I didn't think there was a prospect of being an academic so I followed my father into the law, which was a mistake. But it was something I turned out to be good at, which was also unfortunate, because I stayed in it longer than I should have.

**HB**: Was your father putting pressure on you to go into the law?

**NC**: Not directly, if you know what I mean. It was a sort of class thing. I didn't have the confidence to go straight into being an academic, which I desperately wanted to be.

So I became a lawyer. I became, very quickly, an unhappy lawyer. I was reading Foucault and Derrida, and New Left Review to save my soul.

**HB**: Were you a solicitor or were you a barrister?

**NC**: I was a solicitor.

**HB**: So you weren't doing this in the courts themselves.

**NC**: No, I couldn't perform the law. As someone on the far left with some anarchist sympathies, I couldn't perform the law. The law for me was always a deep social construction. So when I started to read Foucault it felt like a sort of coming home. Nonetheless, I was forced to perform the law in other ways, in a corporate setting, in a big law firm, the largest in the world, called Clifford Chance. I quickly became very unhappy and realized that that type of corporate enactment was completely incompatible with the intellectual person that I was, which I had to deny.

**HB**: How long did you last before you bailed?

**NC**: I qualified for two years then disappeared to the other side of the world for four months. I came back, nonetheless, to law for another five or six years after that.

**HB**: What was the other side of the world?

**NC**: Indonesia. I went to Indonesia for travel. But I had already made up my mind to get out, probably two years before I did, because I went back to the city of London to save as much money as possible so that I could get out.

I was doing music on the side as well, which was the thing that initially saved my soul. By chance, through a music contact, I heard about a Masters in Media and Communications at Goldsmiths College in South London. This was the very first year they had run this cross-disciplinary masters. Because it was a very new subject, probably about 15 years in existence, still not clear of its own boundaries, they had no problem with letting a maverick in who had good results and seemed maybe to have something interesting to say.

**HB**: Did they look at you as a maverick because you were a lawyer or did they look at you as a maverick because you were a lawyer with anarchistic sympathies?

**NC**: They probably didn't believe the claims of anarchistic sympathies. They probably saw me as a lawyer who was out to screw them somehow, but nonetheless, they'd take my money. They realized that I was actually quite committed.

After about three or four months, when I was still doing music, I went to some lectures about the role of the audience by David Morley who eventually became my PhD supervisor. He was the leading person in Britain who was thinking about what audiences do with this thing we call media. What he, along with others, discovered is that you can't read off the impacts of media just by reading the text as a literary theorist or a critic would do. It's actually what we call a determinant moment. There is a moment when the audience is watching, when they may be doing something which is not predicted in the text, which could never have been predicted in the text. When I understood that, I realized that this was a subject with quite a lot of depth.

I have no particular interest in media text. I'm not a film buff particularly, not in a way that's relevant to the work I do. I'm not obsessed with television soap opera. I don't love radio or newspapers to the exclusion of everything else. What I am is someone who's interested in the idea that we can represent the social through text forms that carry a sort of weight, to the extent that they almost become the social for us. That trick, if you like, struck me as very interesting because it draws you into anthropology, sociology, really the theory of how societies work at all. That's where it started for me in about 1994.

**HB**: Let me see if I understand this point, because I think it's important for me not to get lost too early on in the conversation. When you're talking about the audience—the audience vis-à-vis the media and the role of society as a point which had initially attracted you and given you a sense of the depth of the field and so forth—it's almost as if there is a dynamic, two-way street, as it were. It's not as if texts are created and presented to this external world that absorbs them or doesn't absorb them; rather, there is a dynamic coming back from the audience. Is that a fair way to look at it?

**NC**: That's exactly right. It's true that to some degree literary theory —which I was very interested in at that time—had anticipated this. There was some work in Germany and America in the 70s and 80s, which was thinking about the text that implied a certain reader, that the author had a certain reader in mind, and the text created a certain space for the reader to move within. That was a revolutionary move within literary theory at the time, but literary theorists and literary critics, by definition, were not people who were doing a sociology of the actual people who did that reading. So the actualities had to remain unknown to the literary theorists, which is fine, because that's what they were trained to do.

When we got to media texts, which can be read by up to 50 million or even 200 million people at a time, the idea of not actually trying to find out what those 200 million people were doing, or at least what a representative sample of them was doing, was absurd.

**HB**: Somewhat incongruous.

**NC**: People still go on doing it: TV critics and film critics, who read the film as if it speaks for society in a certain way. But it clearly became ridiculous to ignore the audience. There was a bit of a battle in the early days of media studies and film studies, between the old literary way of thinking which said, "A brilliant textual analysis gets you to the heart of the text or the film," and the more sociological sense which said, "That may be true, but it can not in principle get you close to the actuality of what 50 million people do when they're in front of that text." Those two perspectives had to be bridged, so audience studies emerged.

I just so happened to be really lucky to find myself in the institution where the leader, the founder of audience studies, David Morley, was. We got along well, so I started my thesis with him. But being the sort of contrary person that I am, there was no way I was going to do straight audience studies, because I already had a number of doubts about how much one could achieve by studying this particular audience of this particular text at this particular moment in time. More and more, I was looking for new ways, oblique ways, into this phenomenon of the mediation of society.

What difference does it make to the thing we think we know as society, or government, or any of these big abstractions we talk about in the social sciences? Our starting point has to be that these processes work through very complex institutions of mediation, which have their own interests, very particular sites that they speak from, and they make damn sure that someone else doesn't get into the shot or the cutting room. There are tremendous power plays involved in the process of mediation. What difference does it make to a society that it is mediated? My core question of all my work is: how do we do social ontology? How do we think about the things that are the social, that are social in a society where they have to pass through a process we call mediation, which is an abstract way of talking about all the things we call media? That's my core question and I started looking at that from early on under David Morley.

**HB**: It seems to me, as a complete non-expert, that a vital aspect of this relationship between the audience and the media is that, not only is the audience absorbing or not absorbing this material, not only is the audience being more active than that and participating, but there is a self-definition. When you talk about social ontology, there is a sense of, who are we as a society? We are not only reacting to this as active participants; we are, in fact, defining ourselves on a societal level. This, it seems to me, is quite a deep point that you're talking about. Is this what you mean by social ontology, or is this an aspect of it?

**NC**: It's one aspect of it because, certainly, people for more than a century have been encouraged to see themselves as members of the audience, be it the audience for television, for radio, or the readership of a newspaper, or whatever. We're coming to the end of that period because there's a crisis coming to media institutions at the moment, which we'll come back to later. But certainly for a century or more, societies, governments, and corporate advertising, have all been based around the assumption that there was a group of people, more or less definable, who could be called the audience, who were the recipients of the processes of the media industries, and certain types of effects could be assumed from that. For example, basic awareness of what the government was about to do when it was going to go to war, or basic awareness of the key brand and fashion signals of the age. We're coming to the end of that period where that can be assumed, but it used to be assumed.

However, it's more than that. Some people from, let's say, a political economy perspective, perhaps a Marxist view of media—I'm not unsympathetic to Marx, but it's not complete—would say, "Well, that's really enough, because we understand the economic determinants of the media industries. We know what drives them. We know what they have to do to make their profit. They will do it. They do it very well. They will produce the audiences who can then watch the ads, and so on, so the programs can be funded, and this and that."

**HB**: And that's the filter through which one looks at things.

**NC**: Well, that's one easy starting point, and I wanted to react against that as well because the audience perspective always said, "That's not enough because the audiences are maybe doing things that neither the economists, nor the business people, nor the accountants, could predict. They're doing what they're doing. We need to understand that."

There's another level to it too, which is that, as I started to think about what my angle for thinking about media institutions would be—not the text, but the institution that we call the media—I realized that this was much less certain and much less studied: *How is the legitimacy of media institutions itself sustained?* We have, at least until recently—because this has stopped, it's now a big shock for everyone—but until recently, the assumption was that you certainly had a TV; you watched a lot of TV within a certain average level; you may have had radio, and you read a newspaper, and so on; and you were broadly oriented towards whatever was on the media wall. I never really started from that assumption because I was always intrigued by the possibility that you might turn your back to the wall. You might swivel round and pay no attention to the media whatsoever.

I once met a decorator who came to decorate my apartment and I said, *"What media do you watch?"*—this was before I was studying media—and he said, *"I never watch any. I just listen to music. I just put on great music all day and that's it."* He was the only person I had ever met who had that view, who trusted the world enough that he could turn his back to the media wall.

**HB**: Do you still have contact with this decorator? I would hang on to that decorator like grim death.

**NC**: No, I don't. And he was quite a good decorator. But the extreme rarity of that position made me realize, when two or three years later I got into actually writing, that there was something—that the rarity had to be produced. His reaction was a perfectly possible one, but was actually extremely rare. That gave me the clue that media institutions actually have to work very hard to produce the situation where they are our automatic port of call when we want to find out what's going on, what's happening, what's real in society, and so on. That was really the start of my work because I then realized that one could use anthropology and sociology to understand those hidden processes, which the media never wants to talk about. It wants them to be precisely taken for granted. These are processes that actually underlie their legitimacy as media institutions. That was where my work really started, out of that puzzlement.

I found that this had really not been studied because media studies at that point was trying to justify itself by saying, *"This is an academic subject and media are really important."* The discipline had precisely not looked at that foundation because that would have been to expose the very uncertainty that it couldn't expose at that early stage of its formation. But at that point it became possible, so that's what I did.

**HB**: You were right at the threshold, as it were, of the field developing, let's just say, a deeper level of maturity by being able to examine its own roots, by going to the meta-level and saying, *"Well, what actually are these institutions? How do these institutions get into our heads?"*

**NC**: It might sound a bit grand to put it that way, but I think—

**HB**: Well, *I* put it that way.

# Questions for Discussion:

*1. To what extent is it essential to be a "maverick" in order to be genuinely creative?*

*2. Have you ever met anyone like Nick's decorator? Would you say that your consumption of media has increased, decreased, or remained the same over the past 5 years?*

# II. Deconstruction

*Probing the Media*

**NC**: I think what happened was—and some things got a little clearer looking back—I felt the move I was making at that stage seemed almost crazy. People didn't have a clue what I was taking about, partly because I decided that if this process was such a broad one—society-wide basically; it didn't just happen in the media studios, otherwise, how could it affect the rest of society? It had to have been happening everywhere, as Foucault understood power to be happening everywhere—then the range of things one would look at to understand this would be very broad.

In my thesis, for example, I looked at, on the one hand, people going to sites of the filming of TV programs—"pilgrimages", if you like—to the "real" place where it happened, in a crime show, a soap opera, etc. I felt that was a clue to the sense of how place is built through media, this "real" place. On the other hand, I looked at protesters who were not interested in media at all; they were interested in having their voice heard about animal rights, or whatever their cause happened to be. They would go to wherever they needed to be to make that protest, but then the media would come to them, or not, and they would realize what it would take to be in the shot rather than not in the shot. So the media would go from being something entirely intangible and just assumed, to being something extremely real that they fought over, literally, to be in the shot.

**HB**: So, what the metrics are of being there.

**NC**: Yes, literally the metrics and the physical action. They had to act in a certain way if they were going to be in the shot and not the other guy. This meant that in both cases, for totally different reasons, people had to act out and bring to the surface the deep assumptions they had about why media were important and what one had to do to be in this important thing called media.

**HB**: Did they have to bring them to the surface or were they implicit?

**NC**: Well, they were implicit, but when I say "bring to the surface", I'm drawing on a strand of sociology called ethnomethodology, which was developed by Harold Garfinkel. He was looking at the deep underpinning assumptions of social interaction, which never come to the surface because they simply don't need to unless someone disrupts them. Then they have to be brought upon to repair the situation.

I had the instinct that one could do the same in relation to something as deep as media power. It was very hard to get people to talk about, "*Well, why do you switch on the TV at 9 o'clock every evening? Tell me why you do it.*" They say, "*Well, you just do. What else do you expect?*" and so on. But you can draw those answers to the surface, either by disrupting that, by taking people's media away—that wasn't in my power as a researcher. Lecturers sometimes do that with their students in Media Studies 101, which is a good experiment. I did it in a more natural way by studying people who came up to the media apparatus in an unnatural way for the first time. Normally the media is very far away—or, again, at least it was in the pre-mass media era. Now, many media people hold the tools of media in their hands. Things have changed, and we'll come back to that.

Because I had a very broad view of what was relevant to understanding the power of media, initially many people couldn't understand what the hell I was talking about. It turned out that around the same time, in anthropology, some anthropologists were getting more and more interested in media too—Faye Ginsburg in New York and others. They weren't interested in media studies and this text, and how it was produced, and who read it; they had a much more fluid view of how texts circulated and so on, as you'd expect from an anthropologist. They, too, were interested in the social forms that could be built out of that very fuzzy, messy thing called circulating of media. I only realized that commonality around about 2003 or 2004. Then when I looked back, I realized that a number of people who had been doing audience studies and studying media in a broader way were also coming to this paradigm shift: to understand media as a much broader process society-wide.

**HB**: Did you develop active collaborations with some of these anthropologists or sociologists at that point, because it seems like what they're doing is very similar to what you were just describing?

**NC**: I didn't have the chance to develop collaborations. I've actually just come from meeting someone who's an anthropologist here at LSE, who has a similar view of media. Paradoxically, he joined LSE around the time when I was here in 2002 or 2003. He was interested in ritual and knew about my work on the ritual signs of media, but we never met because of the way academic politics worked, I guess.

You need to remember one other thing: at that time—more in Britain than in the United States—media studies was a very dominated field. It had very little confidence in itself.

**HB**: Dominated by whom?

**NC**: Dominated by the rest of the academy. I'm not complaining.

It just was a very new subject dealing with something that many people regarded as quite trashy, not serious, not academically serious. It had to fight quite hard to convince those who were clearly doing serious work in serious disciplines that here was a new subject, a new sort of depth in the social terrain that also had to be taken really seriously. It's fair to say that a lot of sociology, many of the books written in the 70s, 80s, 90s, and even early 2000s, don't even mention media. They were written as if media did not exist. It's only really in the past five or eight years that that has become an impossible starting point.

That complicated things, but it was under those slightly awkward contexts that I developed those ideas about studying media in a much broader way while always trying to hold on to one fundamental point:

not only are media involved in these very broad social effects—for example, when in 1997 Princess Diana died, in Britain people were already saying that attention for mass media was declining because we had lots of TV channels, as if that was going to change everything. People said, *"No, no, you'll never be able to have a big media event anymore."* Princess Diana died and there was a very big media event.

**HB**: It was enormous. Perhaps you can correct me, but it's certainly one of the largest I can remember.

**NC**: It was one of the largest and the way it worked proved to me—I was just a year out from finishing my thesis—it was the most astonishing real world confirmation that I was on to the right sort of line. My prediction was that one could use classical anthropological theory of pilgrimage, of liminality: those moments when we seem to be outside time and place and we seem to be together with each other, close to each other in a more direct way. Victor Turner, the anthropologist, had written about this and called it communitas, special community. It grounds our sense that we're in something, which is society.

There it was happening, in front of my eyes. People were making pilgrimages to a place which stood in for Diana because it was the gates to her London home, Kensington Palace, and they were doing anything they could to touch it, to feel that they had done something that everyone else would recognize as touching this centre. Media reproduced that centre initially, and the circumstances were such that people were really angry with media because they thought the paparazzi who had chased Diana were responsible for her death.

**HB**: They wanted them to think that. There was almost, it seemed to me, a desire to establish a scapegoat.

**NC**: Yes. There were actually good reasons for that. I happened to have been tracking these things a little bit and, by chance, I found that just two or three months before a tabloid newspaper had run a competition for little kids to chase after Diana and take a nice picture.

They gave them £100 and said, "*Great paparazzi. Well done. You've been a good media person.*" Three months later, this was regarded as beyond the pale, as unthinkable aggression, and so on. There was a tremendous double standard about this.

But again, around that moment, when people were chasing cameramen and getting angry with them, the normally completely naturalized mechanism of media—which is so natural that we just look at the world through it; we don't see the frame—was suddenly becoming denaturalized and people were seeing the cameramen and getting angry. This was a remarkable period. It then calmed down, of course, and the re-naturalization happened, and there was the Westminster Abbey service. Everyone then looked through the frame of the television broadcasting again.

That was a confirmation for me that studying media wasn't just a narrow subject, or just an industry interest. What was actually at stake at certain times was society's understanding of itself and the very possibility of going on as a society. That was quite exciting to me, to get that confirmation from the outside, and totally unexpectedly.

**HB**: I want to ask you a question probing this notion of ritual, or pilgrimage in this particular example. Some people might say—I've certainly heard people say—again, using Princess Diana's death as an example, that the reason why there was this overflow of emotion, and these pilgrimages, and this overwhelming societal need to manifest a sense of ritual, is that in our contemporary lives so many of us do not have the sort of rituals that we used to have. People used to go to churches on a regular basis. They used to be participating in a ritualistic life, and through whatever means, they found themselves in a scenario where they had this lack of ritual, to an extent that they might not have even recognized it. Does that ring true to you? Does that have anything to do with reality, and where does media come in to play when it comes to ritual?

**NC**: It's a good question because it's actually quite complicated. I think there is something to that, but it wouldn't get you to the idea, necessarily, that media are the best substitute for religion. Yes, for certain purposes, media operate in a quasi-religious way. We can see the lineaments tracing back to earlier religious practice. However, for me there was always something else at stake in media. We need to remember that media are this massive concentration of symbolic power. If you think very simply what media are—and again, this is not the typical way of looking at media—they are a concentration, within particular institutions, with the power to describe reality. They have the storytelling resources to say, "*This is the way things are for you, for us, for me.*" That's a very valuable resource. It's a resource that's hard to talk about because one of the great skills of those who possess symbolic power is to disguise the fact that they're doing precisely that, and they won't let you have the terms of the critique to take it apart. That's in their power. Symbolic power is enormously important and the most deeply disguised form of power, even more deeply disguised than economic power, I would argue, and certainly more than political power.

Certainly media, to some degree, play a quasi-religious role; we can see that in certain forms. But at the same time, they are in another sort of game, which is holding on to the power to describe reality, holding on to that central social power which they have, that symbolic power. We have to understand the exercise of that power against the background of the societies that we live in where very few people have that power. Very few people have their hands on the resources to tell the story of the world. Very, very few. For most people, that power is absolutely unimaginable and yet—and this is where we get to another side of my work around voice—everyone wants to tell their story in the end. No one wants to die never having told anyone what it's like to be Nick or Howard. Everyone carries a story. That is one of the most important aspects of being human: to carry an account of one's self.

I have sort of a split view in relation to what media do. On the one hand, I'm trying to deconstruct the power operations that are so hard to get at. They are very important to deconstruct because only in that way can you understand why we have certain stories about society, and not others, and what's at stake in them.

**HB**: And what works, presumably.

**NC**: Yes, what works, and if it works, what are the consequences of it working that way and certain other stories never getting told, being too difficult to tell?

Yet, on the other hand, it might seem that one should just be cynical about those who attempt to break in. Let's say, for example, they want to get on to a reality TV show, which is something I came to study more and more in the 2000s. People were trying to break into the media operation by being part of American Idol or whatever show it might be.

But I think it's important not to be cynical about that kind of attempt, because, successful or not, it is an attempt to be recognized. It's an attempt to claim something that is in very short supply: recognition as a valuable human being who carries a story that is worth others receiving.

On the one hand, one needs to deconstruct what is going on and, therefore, see attempts at getting into the media within the context of this massive power structure; and on the other hand, never to minimize what is at stake personally for those trying to carry those things out. It's enormously important.

So I had this double view of the events after Diana died. On the one hand, they could easily be deconstructed from the point of view of anthropology and religion. People were doing exactly what you would expect them to do, to an extraordinary degree. On the other hand, they were also trying to speak. They were also trying to be heard in what, for them, was enormously important and particular: their love for Diana, the importance of Britain today where that type of queen could never be queen, and so forth. It was a very particular message.

**HB**: It was spontaneous as well. That's the other interesting thing.

I'd like to back up a little bit because you mentioned several times that your views were unorthodox, that you were a maverick, and that you were looking at things in different ways than other people were. Media studies was at an earlier stage in its development.

I want to ask you, more specifically, how other people reacted to this. Your supervisor, presumably, would endorse your views, or would endorse your right to have those views at least. Tell me a little bit more about the way other people were looking at media studies at the time, and what that was all about.

**NC**: I was very lucky to have just the right supervisor, who was supportive, who could see something in what I was doing and just let me go. I was also lucky to have an examiner for the thesis, Roger Silverstone, who was one of the very few people studying media at that time who seriously paid attention to anthropology, who had a much broader view of theoretical resources one could draw upon in studying media, and who was interested in ritual. That's why I wanted, fairly quickly, to come to LSE where he was the head of the department.

**HB**: I see. So he influenced you considerably.

**NC**: Yes, he did. Although, for me, he was not always pessimistic enough about the implications, but he was one of the few people who took that side, a side some people might call softer, but it's not soft at all. In reality it's very material and it's very related to power questions.

Just to correct something I said: in a sense, it's true that the approach I was taking was not one that had been common before, and I was one of a number of people involved in, almost without us even knowing it, shifting the terrain. But that only became possible because the foundations of the field had been laid quite quickly in the first 10 or 20 years with really good analyses of the production of media, the economics of that, analyses of how media texts work and their semiotic complexity. Then with David Morley there were really good studies of what audiences do in front of these texts. Those were the building blocks.

Once they were in place, in the mid-90s, many people in the field were thinking, Well, where next? The audience is actually infinitely complex. They could be watching one of 10 channels. Which one do we follow? Little did we know what level of complexity was going to come in the 2000s, let alone the 2010s. Already people were getting worried by complexity, so they started to argue, for example, that the audience was undecidable; one has to go out into space and somehow pick up the signals of media influence in other ways. There were clear problems with that. It was going nowhere. We needed new angles, which were sharp and definite enough to get at the enormity of the topic, the power of media institutions, which somehow took for granted, but went beyond, the older approaches. I guess that's, in a sense, what I was doing. So, it was in no way rejecting those earlier approaches; it was building on top of them a new and broader way of thinking about media. I think probably all my work has been trying to do that from various angles and I'm lucky that I came at the right time, rather than the wrong time.

Also, the most important point of all is that the whole media ecology and environment was changing profoundly from the late 90s to the early 2000s. The Internet was starting to be known. People were starting to realize it wasn't just an occasional eccentricity; it would become a regular, and then a dominant part of everyday life, until now, when we struggle to find a moment of time when we're not, in some way, connected, and this might be problematic, as we'll get to later. The world has almost overtaken those limitations of media studies to the point that we can't always imagine those early—

**HB**: It's almost inverted completely.

**NC**: Yes, it's almost inverted. And we've lived with that and we're trying to understand what's going on now.

I've given you that story because it gives you a sense of how what now seems blindingly obvious had to be fought for a little bit at one point. It gradually became possible to say a bit more in public, and then that became the norm. Now, the norm is so complex that we're bewildered about how to understand the complexity.

# Questions for Discussion:

*1. Do you think that the evolution of the media landscape over the past 10–15 years represents changes in degree or in kind?*

*2. To what extent does "perfect deconstruction" require "perfect objectivity"?*

# III. Investigating Power
*Political and economic issues*

**HB**: Let me move to political power. You've alluded to it several times during the course of the first stage of this conversation. It does not strike me as terribly surprising, based upon your comments so far and what I know about your work, that you would be interested in critiquing certain aspects of power and certain types of power. But I can see that it might be confusing to people who think, *Why is this media studies guy all of a sudden writing about neoliberalism? Who does he think he is?* and so forth. Tell me a little bit about that book and about your work in that particular area more generally, what you were trying to achieve, what the responses were, and whether you thought you achieved it.

**NC**: Let me give you just a bit of background. Although most of my work has been around media—that's the problem, the object I am most interested in—I was also pretty taken early on with cultural studies, as it's still known, particularly the strand of cultural studies that came from the great literary theorist and sociologist of literature, Raymond Williams, who was Professor of Drama at Cambridge in the early 60s and 70s. He had a very special vision of why you should study media at all, and why you should study everyday cultural processes at all. His idea was that, in democracies that are very far from perfect, where there is a massive gap between the diagram of how democracy should work and the messy forms of exclusion— normally exclusion, but occasionally inclusion—that is the reality, you needed a much broader subject that could listen for that gap and the forms that it got translated into in terms of everyday politics or everyday cultural response, and so on. His notion was cultural studies.

Cultural studies, like media studies, has also been attacked for many purposes, and often rightly. It's gone into an obscure jargon, which is very unhelpful. But that core vision, that the project of creating a democratic culture is deeply incomplete—which actually has quite a bit in common with someone like John Dewey from political theory—that has always guided my work. I have written some books, which are trying to tap into that while not specifically emphasizing the media, but instead emphasizing the deeper patterns of exclusion and inclusion in culture. That was the side of my work that I turned to when I wrote the book about voice, *Why Voice Matters*, in the late 2000s.

The specific motive for writing it was a common concern to so many people at the time: despair at the apparently closed political discourse of the Blair government in Britain and the Bush government in the United States, and the seemingly inescapable conclusion that there were no realities but market realities. There was no way of building adequate politics except by starting with what markets happened to require and want. This, for me, was unacceptable. It excluded all the types of politics that I was interested in. Not because I'm against markets. Of course, I'm not against markets.

**HB**: I wanted to clarify that. I can imagine this being one of two possible scenarios. On the one hand, this could be: I believe X and the powers that be deny X completely, and therefore I think it's important to have my view presented. Or it could be: There really are many different ways of approaching problems. Things are much more sophisticated, much more complicated. There are many avenues to explore. Historians, political philosophers, dramatists, literary figures, and so forth, have depicted all sorts of tensions within society for centuries, and all of a sudden these guys who are running our government are ignoring everything that has happened in the past 300 years other than the one particular ideological strand that fits their purposes. I think, for the benefit of society, we should ensure that people are at least made aware of what's going on and that there be broader choice. I am guessing it was the second one.

**NC:** You're right and you've given a much nicer account of the second one than the first. It was the second, and I think it was the second for an important reason.

There has been a lot of—often media-based, but also cultural—deconstruction of standard power plays, whether Marxist or whatever. They exist. They're fine. But that's not what I set out to be doing as an academic. I thought I could take them as a given. I was always trying to find a different way that would get to the underlying conditions of those power plays. So with respect to my work on the media, it was the underlying conditions of the legitimacy of media institutions which underlie the particular games they play. But in the cultural area, my strength is definitely not looking at and deconstructing particular political ideologies. I'm not a political scientist. I'm not a political critic. What I wanted to get to the bottom of was the sense of disempowerment that I felt and a number of people around me felt. The values we thought were the starting points for politics—for us the only ones, but certainly at least possible starting points for politics, around communities, solidarity, possibly some measure of greater equality in society, voice, recognizing people as valid human subjects—were suddenly being trumped by a different set of values that could never hear those earlier values, that would literally erase them, or efface them.

As I said, I'm not against markets at all. I agree with Amartya Sen when he said, "*Markets were often very good. They are a form of social experiment that has been immensely liberating in so many societies.*" I certainly don't disagree with that. What I am against is the ideology that markets, in the way they function, provide the only model for how society, something different, should function and, therefore, the only model for how politics should regulate how societies should function. At least two big leaps are being made in that sentence.

That was the trick which Milton Friedman, in trying to initially push a different notion of economics, but make it speak very loudly to government as well, for society and politics, played in the 1970s. I was very struck when I looked back at one of his books, one of his more popular books; he says at the beginning of it how isolated he had been at the beginning when he had developed these ideas of giving total freedom to markets and stripping down the state completely. He decided that for any change to come you had to have the right resources lying around, the right ideas in place somewhere because someone could grab them. He said, "I'm writing this book so those ideas are now somewhere around."

**HB**: "Here are the resources. Eventually this idea will prevail."

**NC**: "Someone's going to listen to this someday," and then by the second edition he had already influenced Thatcher and Reagan.

I decided to write that sort of book, a book that would put some resources on the table, that under some political circumstances— maybe not immediate ones—could be used. It was my most personal book to date so I was trying to get to something that I could hold on to as someone who felt politically in despair at that point in the mid-2000s.

I decided it would be about the basic value of voice. Not the fact of voice, because as many people pointed out to me, everyone's got voice today. By the time I had finished the book everyone had a blog, everyone had a phone, and so on. Of course voice is everywhere.

**HB**: But that's really, in a way, your point. It's about the denial of other voices. This ideology, if I understand you correctly, involves an exclusionary principle, the exclusion of a wide variety of different voices. Your argument, it seems to me, is not so much, "My voice is the right one." Obviously you think your voice is the right one. Everyone thinks his or her voice is the right one. Rather, you are subscribing to a larger-picture view that it is essential for your voice to at least be heard, or contended with, or appreciated as existing.

**NC**: Yes, that's right. And there's a problem here, which someone who's critical of voice will raise. They'll say, "Well, not everyone can be heard. Society is complex. You need all sorts of controlling of resources, and so on." No one would sensibly deny that. Taking that to the next level, if we start from the principle that voice has to be respected in principle, but it can't always be delivered all the time; then we have to think about the organizational ways in which things can be done, taking account of that value. The problem for me in the neoliberal project was not necessarily that particular groups of people were denied voice—although that may be true as well—but that the very principle of giving weight to voice was overridden by the idea of market functioning. If you imagine the simple cases of corporate takeovers, the mere fact that the markets have decided, due to stock market prices and other things, that this company just had to take over this other one, means that there simply was no issue about whether the voices of the human individuals working for the second company should be registered anywhere in that process. One didn't compute into the other.

**HB**: Because it was a higher prioritization. The market dogma was at a higher level and you can't possibly even conflict with that.

**NC**: It wouldn't translate. They were just totally different types of things. When you think about it, this is a notion of markets as the best model for understanding social order, and therefore political order, that goes back to the early 19th century. It was Michel Foucault in his amazingly prescient lectures on neoliberalism in the early 80s who spotted this.

This deeper notion of market fundamentalism, which doesn't just say markets are important—it even says, crazily, markets never fail which is, of course, false—is grounded in a much deeper idea: that we can't believe they fail. We can't take that into account because markets are the only real possible order for human complex living.

**HB**: So it's axiomatic at some level.

**NC**: It's axiomatic and that's what Friedman and so many others tried to achieve. That led to all sorts of flowering: of rational choice theory as an understanding of society, rather than just of people playing games in markets.

I was trying to get at what was wrong with that when applied as a political doctrine. This was around the time when the Blair government, alongside Bush of course, was making privatization not just an exciting experiment, as it had been with Thatcher, but literally the only norm for running public services. Common resources remained at the public good but could now only be run—for reasons of "rationality or, even worse, "modernity"—on the basis of market functioning. I thought there was something deeply wrong with this, but it was clearly not enough to just argue with the political dogma. That was, itself, hard enough and, in fact, we still haven't got away from that. I wanted to get at the values that underpinned it.

I turned to a number of sources. I turned to philosophical writers for whom our need as human individuals to carry an account of ourselves, to have that account recognized by others, and to be recognized as people with such an account, was so fundamental that we couldn't really imagine a culture worth living in without that value being respected. I stayed with those sorts of writers and built that into a broader theory. I was also delighted to find common cause with a writer such as the development economist Amartya Sen, who in one sense would appear to be a very mainstream figure because he's listened to by the World Bank and—

**HB**: Well, he has won the Nobel Prize. When you win the Nobel Prize, you get listened to by people.

**NC**: But he's actually an extremely radical figure because, from early in his career, he has always insisted that economics made a deep mistake around the 1810s and 1820s, when the double science that Adam Smith had, the science of moral sentiments and the science of understanding how markets work, got split apart and the latter just became economics. Amartya Sen insists that that has to be put back together again, that we always need an ethical critique of how our approaches to what we call the economy—which is just our ways of doing things together with resources—translate into particular ways of life, which may or may not be good lives. He started raising the ethical question again.

That's sort of why I wrote that book. It was an experimental book in the sense that I didn't expect to be heard by economists. I hoped possibly to be heard by a few politicians. That didn't happen, even though I rushed the book out for the 2010 election. It survived at most as a leaflet at one conference, but disappeared.

But it has had a longer-term impact because people have said to me they wanted to hear someone making that sort of case.

**HB**: And that's presumably what you wanted. You really wanted a longer-term impact, right? It's nice to have impacts all over the place, but if you had to choose, I'm guessing a longer-term impact is what you were aiming for.

**NC**: Absolutely. Because I think the only way one can change such a profound shift in thinking as occurred in the 70s and 80s is through the longer term, through validating other forms of value. It's a book not so much about voice, but about the project of really valuing voice, and meaning it, and organizing society on that basis, or at least partly on that basis, and not on the basis that markets are all that matter.

**HB**: I want to explore that a little bit because you've isolated, I think, a real issue in any modern functioning state, which is that there is a plethora of different voices, of different people, of different interests, and yet, at the same time, to be efficient, to be effective, you have to have a sense of coherence. You have to have a clear sense of the government of the day being able to enact, in some reasonably rigorous way, its views, which means that not every voice will be heard constantly, not every voice will be paid attention to. So how do you balance those two things? You've highlighted the tension between them. Clearly ignoring every single other voice that is counter to your own and labelling it as philosophically bankrupt and saying that your views are axiomatic, is not the way to go. That's an extreme view whether your view is neoliberalism, or communism, or whatever. It doesn't really matter. If you are anathematizing every other view but your own, that, I think, is not an intellectually responsible approach.

On the other hand, the other extreme would be to say, "Well, I'm just the representative of the people. So we're going to have an Internet vote on every single decision of the day. We're going to listen to all the voices all the time," and so forth. That's not a terribly coherent way to precede either. How do you balance these two things?

**NC**: No one is near to finding a solution to this. I think the problem is not just to do with neoliberalism. There is an overlapping problem which takes us back to the media side of my work and the growing complexity of society, which is that, partly through the success of media industries, all of us are more and more getting used to, at least the idea that we might have a voice and it might be picked up somewhere. That may not be what happens in reality, but the idea is not as strange as it would have been in 1860, let alone 1560.

That's creating enormous problems for democratic institutions because they're becoming less and less legitimate. They are also less and less able to control the flows of information about themselves, because of the digitization of information. This is making all institutions very unstable. The sustaining of democratic institutions is very difficult.

At the same time, because of this political force to actively exclude certain types of voice—traditionally the voices of trade unions and other forms of voice which interrupt market functioning—you've got a political reason why people are angry, why they felt cut out of the political process and that they're not being listened to. For various reasons, there is a need for political institutions to rethink themselves—I would argue that there is reason for all institutions to rethink themselves—so that they are more adequate for the possibilities of representation which now exist in a digital age. They're a long way from rising to that challenge. A value of voice won't be enough to get you there, because that only gets you started down the road.

**HB**: But it's a start.

**NC**: It's a start and I think a second start would be to say that we're restructuring an area of society, or industry, or whatever. It's not sufficient to simply say that the market solution is enough.

We have to look at whether that will match what the bulk of people affected by the process will want, and what the appropriate mechanisms for listening to them would be, which will be complex. That's the third stage. We need to think much more sophisticatedly about what the adequate mechanisms are for registering voice in a much more complex and flat society. I say "registering" because it's clearly not the same thing as literally everyone being heard all the time, because then no one can be heard.

There is very little work on this. I'm interested, for example, in the work of a legal writer like Beth Noveck from the United States, who was Obama's e-government advisor in the early days of his first administration. She wrote a book called Wiki Government. It's a very insightful book and a very unusual book because in it she points out that not only do digital tools create possibilities for lots of people to speak; they actually create a challenge for institutions of government. They could actually refigure themselves. They could have different groups of experts created online for different topics. They're failing to do that. She argues they need to rethink their legit-imacy and organizational structure so that they allow that possibility, in a way that doesn't undermine government totally, but will involve a reconfiguration of its authority. These are very complicated changes, needless to say.

In writing the book about voice I was only pointing in a direction. With the Euro crisis from 2008 to 2010, the global financial crisis, and the massively complex problems that all governments had to deal with after that, it's not surprising that we haven't had much success in dealing with these underlying nuts and bolts issues about how government can remain legitimate in the longer term.

**HB**: But these nuts and bolts issues are very long-term issues. If you take the very long-term view of democracy, the modern democratic project, from roughly the 18th century onwards, these things don't happen overnight. One of the things that has certainly stimulated me while listening to you talk and also having thought about these things a little bit before myself, is an exploration of how much our modern organs of the state do depend on technology and the technology of their time.

There are different ways of looking at democracy. You can look at it as an active project or you can look at it as a feasible project. You can say, "Look, in Periclean Athens everyone went down to the agora and voted. We can't do that now because we have 300 million people in this particular country and we don't have an agora big enough for all of them." But, on the other hand, you can say, "Hang on. We actually do have the tools. We can actually consult the people. But do we want to be consulting the people?"

When representative democracy was first formulated, on the one hand there was a sense that this system was just feasible, that you can't run a country any other way. If you were living in what were then the thirteen colonies of the United States, at the time, you had to send your representative to Washington because you couldn't possibly consult all the people. So there was a practical need to have representative democracy.

Nowadays, you can say, "We don't actually have that practical need anymore. Is that the best system? Do we actually want to do that because we trust the judgment of particular individuals to reflect the greater good of the body politic?" I think these are questions whose time has come to be reflected upon and re-reflected upon again. Technology is really a catalyst, it seems to me, to be able to do this, and books like yours and ideas like those of Beth Noveck, are really interesting spurs for us to rethink the mechanisms of how we govern ourselves and why we do things in the way that we do.

To some extent, I think the global economic crisis is a bit of a distraction. Of course it's there, and of course if you're involved in it, and of course if you're the government at the time, you are concerned about it. But the larger issue, if you take the longer view, is what are governments doing in the 21st century? What do we mean by democracy? What do we mean by a functioning state? What do we mean by exporting democracy? What democracy do we export? How should we govern ourselves? These are fundamental societal issues.

I'm encouraged by the fact that people are coming at this from different angles, but it seems to me that you're almost a little bit defensive when you talk about these issues; it's as though you're saying, "Okay, I'm a media studies guy. I'm saying this stuff about democracy. I've got my views. Somebody who's in the Obama administration has different views about this. Yes, this really is important and people should listen to me. Politicians ignored me. A couple of economists paid attention to me." But it seems to me this is something that really should be part of the social consciousness now. I would like more people to be discussing this. Who better to lead the discussion than somebody who's actually thinking about how societies and media interact? Maybe "media" is the wrong word, but it seems to me that if we're thinking about how best to govern ourselves, who better to listen to than somebody who's looking at how we evaluate information and how we process information. Do you agree with this or am I just completely off topic?

**NC**: Well, I don't know if I'm being defensive. Perhaps I'm being defensive in the sense that I'm deliberately reflecting in order to explain the history of the field that I'm coming from, a field that, for a long time, has been in a defensive position vis-à-vis the traditional sciences, and that's a fact. That affects our whole field.

Personally, I don't feel at all defensive about these questions of value, for the reasons you state. The idea that it would be better to organize our way of doing things together, on the basis that the accounts we each have of our lives should be taken into account in the organization of things, is, I think, probably one of the only bases on which we can imagine a livable life together. It is fundamental. Of course, it's breached all the time, in war and other power plays, but it is fundamental. As the philosopher Paul Ricoeur said, *"A culture without narrative, without the possibility of carrying one's story, is literally not a culture, i.e. it's unlivable."* Yet, that was the promise of neoliberalism, and it's been enacted in many, many different forms.

I wouldn't agree with you that the financial crisis is completely irrelevant, because I think—

**HB**: I don't think I said it was completely irrelevant.

**NC**: No, but you know what I mean. You said that compared to the other big stuff we can discount it a bit, and in some ways that's right. But there was something very particular about what happened with the financial crisis, particularly through the knock-on effect on the Euro crisis in southern Europe. After only two years, even after the nostrums of neoliberalism (that markets will always deliver and they will never fail) had been comprehensively proven to be false, and admitted so even by someone like Alan Greenspan; nonetheless, they were still being put into practice to override the democracies of Greece, Portugal, Spain, and Italy. This was not on the basis that this was exactly what the politicians wanted; there was no hostility to democracy, but on the basis of logic, on the basis that this is the way things have to be.

**HB**: This is the axiomatic thing again.

**NC**: And on the basis of the markets deciding if, for example, Greece is ready for the challenge or not. This notion of the markets deciding has a perfectly respectable logic of its own. But the massive expansion of global capital and financial markets—and it's an expansion of really millions of folds since the late 70s and, particularly, the late 80s when market trading was liberalized—has meant that there is this colossal deficit affecting all countries. It will affect America when, or if, its currency comes under threat from the Chinese renminbi at some point in the future. Then we will certainly hear about it as a problem, assuming America still has some influence over global media at that point. This is a problem affecting every society. The structure of global capital and the transfer of resources enabling ordinary things to go on everywhere in sync, is incompatible with delivering the choice and the possibility of having an influence over their own economy, the very economy of those people. No one has yet worked out how to do that. It is a really deep problem.

You could also look more positively at a version of the same problem in relation to global warming. Clearly most people think something needs to be done. It's very complex. There's a great deal of uncertainty about exactly what should be done. Where things should be decided is deeply problematic. Is it the national level? Is it the global level? Is it at the level of local communities where people can change certain things quickly? And they might as well get on with changing those things quickly and be given power to do so on that basis that the problem is insoluble at higher levels. Even a problem like that—I say "even a problem like that", but it's perhaps the biggest problem facing humanity today—raises questions about the level at which democracy should work and the timescale at which it needs to work.

I was very interested to read a political theorist like Pierre Rosanvallon from France who wrote a book about democratic legitimacy a year or two ago. He argued that the different timescales of democracy—the timescale of the election every four or five years and the timescale on which things need to be checked to know that the solutions are still legitimate for the people being affected—they are out of sync. He points out that the early theorists of democracy were on to this about three years after the French Revolution. They didn't have a solution then and somehow the problem was forgotten in the wash of history.

**HB**: It wasn't a good time three years after the French Revolution.

**NC**: No, no it wasn't. They had a few other things to think about. But, staggeringly, they had spotted that problem already from the beginning, as he points out. We haven't solved it yet, and we are going to have to gradually move towards solutions.

That then takes us to the question of what the media can contribute. Some of what I've been talking about might, in some sense, sound anti-media. But I've never wanted to be anti-media. I just wanted to expose the power sources on which they rely so we can understand them better. I think, paradoxically, some of the things that media can do—give voice, witness suffering, particular suffering in particular places, and play it back to governments who don't want to hear it—remains extremely important and needs to be held on to even as market pressures within the media industries make it more and more difficult to deliver exactly that essential function.

# Questions for Discussion:

*1. What role do you think that the corporate ownership structure of media plays in the content associated with that media?*

*2. How do you think that the rise of China as an economic superpower will impact media both in China and beyond?*

# IV. The Future of Media

*Ruminations and speculations*

**HB**: How do you see the future of media? We've talked about this a little bit. You've alluded to how media has changed, what has happened because of the Internet, how it is constantly changing, how it may have, in fact, reached a tipping point or even gone past a tipping point. What are your fearless predictions for the next five or ten years?

**NC**: There is no one who wouldn't fear giving predictions.

**HB**: Okay. Then what are your fearful predictions?

**NC**: Let me give you the size of the problem and then perhaps you'll see why I think it's beyond prediction. That's the view of most people in the media industry at the moment. No one knows where things are going. On the one hand, you have a massive expansion of the things we call media—the platforms, the processes, the ways of receiving things that we call media—from three or four simple forms, which still exist of course, to any number of other entry points, all of which can be linked together and linked back to the old media in sort of unpredictable feedback loops.

It's gotten to the point where, a few years ago, The Economist wrote, "No one knows what a media company is anymore." In a sense that's true, because we now consider the leading media companies to be things like Google, which doesn't make media; Facebook, which is a platform that doesn't make media but allows us to make our own media; YouTube; Twitter; and so on.

**HB**: The Economist itself used to be owned by Pearson Group, which you wouldn't necessarily think of as a media company.

**NC**: Exactly. So what media is, is very uncertain.

Secondly, coming out of that multiplicity is an even deeper uncertainty. This goes right back to that fundamental point we started with, about, causally speaking, the special moment of the audience. What are people doing with media? It becomes maximally more uncertain because there are so many things they could be doing, and there are so many more relations between the things they're doing. Exponentially the complexity grows.

We're now in a phase, I think, where people genuinely are doing new things which we don't have easy words for. In my recent book, I try to capture some of these things. To give you a simple example, the idea of showing or pointing used to be very simple: I would point my finger at an interesting book, or cake, or what have you, and you would look at it or go and sample it, and I've communicated with you. That's a simple ostensive act. Now, if I'm sitting in London and you're in Los Angeles, and I find a link to an interesting article, I can, without comment, point you to that by simply sending you the link. You read it a minute later in Los Angeles and I've pointed to that thing. This is an astonishing extension of a very, very simple act that is basic to human communication.

Similarly, the act of simply showing that I've just done something could easily slip into the flow of history and disappear. But now, I might have recorded it and I can show it to you wherever you are in the world. In fact, I can show it to a million people at once. Every moment can be replayed on different levels in any combination and so on. These are extraordinary changes in basic possibilities of action.

**HB**: What do you think this all means? What do you think it implies on a societal level?

**NC**: It's certainly not leading to a massive shift in power, because these new resources are precisely the ones that, at some level, big institutions are trying to get some control of. Of course they can't control what we do on YouTube or Facebook. That's not their interest. But controlling the platform, controlling the terms and conditions of the platform, is something they're very interested in, because they are interested in the data value of what we do, and I'll come back to that.

From our point of view as users, this is creating uncertainty. Although we are now in a grounded situation—we're talking to each other in a very focused way and we're recording our conversation for a specific purposes—I don't know for certain that you don't have a phone in your pocket and you're recording my voice for other purposes, which you will shortly tweet.

**HB**: I do have a phone in my pocket, but I'm not going to do any of that.

**NC**: I'm sure. And you don't know I'm not doing the same. We don't know there aren't other people listening through the wall. We don't know what will happen to this image when you put it on the website and it may be circulated in places none of us could predict.

**HB**: There's a loss of control at some level.

**NC**: Yes. And this is a radical shift in the boundaries of communication situations, far beyond just televising. It's that the boundaries are, in principle, now porous, in ways that we don't fully understand, because it depends on contingencies that are not in our control.

One question I think we're all asking now when we are in a communicative situation is: Where is this? It's not the same as it was before we had digital communication.

Similarly, because of the storing of information, we all now wonder: When is this? We are now in a time when if I say something silly during this conversation and it's stored on your website and listened to, I may never escape. Even in 20 years' time it could be coming back to haunt me in a way that was pretty unlikely in the past, unless I made the effort of inscribing something in a book that was printed.

Out of that comes the bigger problem of, what is the order in the situation? Which type of institution ultimately has more control than others over the circulation of this type of information, its weight, whether it gets heard or not, whether it gets washed away by other information, and so on? Questions of order and power are much more difficult now.

In terms of where this is going, I don't have any answers about the exact forms things are going to take. Anyone who could predict the next social media platform would either be extremely rich and silent, or they would be a fool and speaking.

But the idea that there will be some social media platforms, something with a lineage that we will recognize and be able to trace back to where we are now—clearly this is a very important form that has emerged in the past five to six years and is going to continue in some form with or without various constraints.

We have the beginnings of an architecture we're starting to understand and I think it's raising some deep ethical questions. I think these are the questions that are now becoming interesting.

**HB**: Are there privacy issues? Is that one of the concerns? I'm thinking of people like Edward Snowden. I'm dating myself in terms of the "when" question that you discussed earlier.

**NC**: Well, I don't think he'll be forgotten for some time. Privacy is one of the issues. Privacy implies that we have something that we would assume to be private and there is a problem when it's made more public.

I think we're in an even more troubled situation now. If you look at Facebook, for example, we are now often communicating with each other in a situation where we're not quite sure who we're communicating with and we're not quite sure of the parameters in which what we do will be used. It's no longer clear. That's just one example of the quandaries we're now facing.

If we think of the issue around data, which gets us into Snowden territory—I would like to stress the corporate side of it, rather than the state side, because this is not just about the big, bad state. This is about the whole infrastructure of surveillance, which is now the norm, which involves corporations as much as, if not more than, states. That is leading us to a situation where literally everything we do, every fibre of action in the texture of our lives, is a data source and, therefore, a value source for corporations, provided it happens on the platforms where we're encouraged to spend our time. No one knows what reaction there will be to this in the longer term. There were shrieks of pain over certain things but that subsides back into the banal normality of media, as always happens with media. Yet, I think we're beginning to get to a point where the costs of this infrastructure, of being constantly connected—which is, on the face of it, a good thing—are so high that we may have rather unpredictable conflicts and unpredictable fractures.

**HB**: Such as?

**NC**: Well, we don't know what form they're going to take. Facebook fears that for groups under a certain age demand is falling for their product. But there will be other platforms, some of them with less surveillance than others.

I don't know exactly what form this will take. Media infrastructure up until the late 80s was a relatively straightforward bounded thing. You either had a TV or you didn't. You either had five channels or one. Maybe you had radio. And you either read a newspaper or you didn't. Now everyone is somehow in a universe of interconnected meaning and the price of being in that universe is, more or less, to be tracked. These companies depend on that to reach others because mass communication and personal communication are now overflowing in the same space. The option of being completely without a phone or completely without any form of Internet resource is pretty limiting.

**HB**: Unless you're an interior decorator.

**NC**: Right. I haven't seen him recently. I would be interested to know what type of smartphone he now has, maybe one with only music apps on it. I don't know.

But the options of opting out are very limited because we have acquired a communications infrastructure, an information infrastructure, which is massively sophisticated, whose workings none but the most sophisticated technical elites can understand, an infrastructure whose interrelations are absolutely opaque.

I was very struck by a book, by a legal theorist named Julie Cohen, called *Configuring the Networked Self.* She argued that there was something deeply authoritarian about this infrastructure, not because there was any political intent on the part of those doing it; they were just trying to make value—

**HB**: But authoritarianism emerges somehow.

**NC**: Authoritarian in the sense that we have no choice but to accept it, as she puts it.

**HB**: And participate at some level.

**NC**: Yes, because we have to operate, and we have to operate through this. There are very few alternative macro-infrastructures and the price of using it is participation in some sense, generating data from which value can be created. I think she's right. I think, though we're only at the beginnings of the opening of this horizon, there is something troubling about the ethics of this.

I don't think it's any accident that in the past five or six years, more and more writers—initially on the margins, perhaps—have started to raise ethical questions about our life in media. They're not like the voices of the 1970s and 80s crying in the wilderness saying, "Junk your TV!" They're not preaching. They're simply troubled by the quality of the lives we're now leading, which are so intensely mediafied, and the costs that has for us, our bodies, and our personal relationships.

For example, Sherry Turkle who wrote the book *Alone Together*; she was one of the first proselytizers of being online, being on screen. She's deeply troubled by where this has come to. Or Jaron Lanier, the founder of virtual reality in the early 1990s, wrote a book called *You*

*Are Not a Gadget*, in which he argued that there are human values which are being trashed and overwritten by a bet entirely on infra-structures that count, measure, and create value, and leave little place for consultation or for time off the network.

**HB**: Are these just voices in the wilderness or are these part of a growing counterculture that will have a larger and larger effect?

**NC**: I think they're not voices in the wilderness because both of them are very significant figures, who were originally on the inside of the development of computing and its embedding in our lives, who are now speaking out very strongly.

Also, the novelist Dave Eggers. His novel called *The Circle* is a powerful satire on the grand, partly self-deluding, claims of an imaginary mega-media corporation, which is trying to get total data about everyone on the planet and link it up in such a way that our lives online become remarkably simple, but the only price is that everything we do is tracked.

# Questions for Discussion:

*1. What do you think are the principal lessons to be learned from "the Snowdon affair"? Are they any different today than they were 5–8 years ago?*

*2. How has government surveillance, real or potential, impacted our sense of liberty? Readers with a particular interest in this issue are referred to Chapter 4 of **Quest for Freedom** with Queen Mary University of London intellectual historian Quentin Skinner.*

# V. Ever Onwards

*Listening to alarms, big data and making a difference*

**HB**: So if I'm reading this and I'm alarmed, what can I do about this? You're portraying this horrible dystopia in which our lives are controlled. We're forced to participate by this totalitarian or tyrannical combination of media or devices. We have to be in this connected world. We have so little time for reflection. We extrapolate from where we are today and the angst that we have today, which makes such a cruel mockery out of these potential happy days in the future that were reported when I was a small child, like when people would say things like, *"What are we going to do with all of our leisure time?"* Now, of course, we're in this scenario where people are feeling increasingly pressured. They're feeling increasingly connected in a way which they're not necessarily desirous of, but they feel that they have to be. They're mediating their experiences in ways which are much less direct and much less personally rewarding than they might otherwise be. And they're alarmed. So what do we do about it?

**NC**: Well, the first thing is to listen to the alarm. Don't discount it. Don't pretend it's unimportant, or illegitimate, or it's not what's expected. Stay with it. Listen to it carefully. Listen to the values that are implicit in that alarm and the other possibilities which you have less time for, which you are in practice discounting all the time when you give time to being online and being on Facebook. Think about those other possibilities.

Clearly it's not a matter of just walking away and turning our back on social media. The power of social media platforms to draw people together very fast, to go to a place they don't yet know, for a topic they're not yet clear about, within the next hour, to then cause an impact on the government, is astonishing. It's a new form and the French revolutionaries would have loved to have had it. But they did their best with pamphlets and posters on walls, and so on.

We can't turn our back on that power but we have to think about where the underlying control over those resources and infrastructures is stored, whether there are any other ways for a broader range of people to get control of that. That will require new forms of activism which we haven't yet seen. They will have to emerge in the future.

I think the third thing that's very important to think about is that we should be aware of states, or corporations, or any other type of organization that has real power over you—in terms of taking away your passport, or stopping you doing business, or drawing taxes—beware when they themselves are very happy to draw on this infrastructure to enhance their power.

I think a lot of the debate around Snowden was phony in the sense that it claimed that the only problem was the big, bad state, forgetting that the much bigger problem is the rise of corporate surveillance, which is, in fact, the model on which states are now increasingly relying. The British government has recently decided to phase out its national census on the basis that it won't in the future need to count its population every 10 years. It now realizes that there would be little point, because now, for a price, much more detailed data are available from the corporate sector all the time.

**HB**: Because of the advertising revenue, they already have all this information.

**NC**: Exactly. Governments who want big data about society can rely on big marketing data—which is the phrase of Acxiom, the leading data collection company in the world—and that reorients the state, in a way. This is what I'm more worried about, but this is what has to be, not feared, but seen as an explicit possibility. There is a risk that states, along with corporations—it seems innocent in the case of corporations; it's definitely not innocent in the case of the state—will increasingly see the very possibility of government having some greater level of power in an ordered space as depending on permanent surveillance from all directions without consent, or with consent that's basically meaningless.

**HB**: It's like agreeing to these terms and conditions when you're trying to log on to the Wi-Fi somewhere. You just want to make sure your Internet connection works, so you just agree to whatever.

**NC**: You have no choice. In that sense it's authoritarian, as Julie Cohen says.

When we get to that stage, where that seems to be the only way of governing, then we're not in neoliberalism; we're in something different. We are in a sort of de facto authoritarianism, which is built out of the organizing properties of very powerful information infrastructures. This is what we all want, in some way. They've been massively freeing and exciting, but, because they're so large, they also have a dark side, which is very dangerous and costly, unless we develop languages and values that acknowledge the danger and start to talk about that as a common project.

There is not a lot of work on this. I think it's a very new issue. I've found that in opening up these sorts of questions to students, they're extremely responsive because this is something that people do want to talk about. But it is not the main thing the governments are talking about.

**HB**: And where will they talk about it? This brings me to an issue that we've skirted around a little bit. It starts as a question about what media studies is, but then there is the question of how these voices are going to get heard and what role media studies—or whatever you would like to call it—will play in that development.

**NC**: With regard to your first point about disciplinary boundaries, they still remain important to some degree. Media studies is an interdisciplinary space. People come to it from all sorts of different backgrounds, sociology in my case; others come from psychology, or political science, or anthropology, or what have you. What brings these people together is a common set of problems, which, as I've tried to bring across, are very deep problems about how the institutions we call media are actually deeply implicated in new projects for organizing society, by many parties including governments and corporations.

It's a problem about the very possibility of social order, as well as democratic political order. Not surprisingly, people across many disciplinary boundaries are now interested in those things: the digital media instruments, platforms, ways of storing data on which those platforms depend, ways of gathering metadata, and so on. Many different people are interested in that so now it becomes irrelevant whether your background was initially IT, literary theory, or philosophy. If you care about those deep questions and are interested in clear ways of formulating questions that speak across all disciplinary boundaries, then you're interested in the same sort of field as I am.

I'll give you an example. This Friday, within LSE, we are setting up a law and communications research network. We're going to see where it goes. That came out of a simple conversation that I had with a professor in the law department, in which he showed me the reading list for his course, and these were the very same books that I was thinking were important to tell my students about. Of course, he does other stuff that I wouldn't do and vice versa, but the core books, the books which are opening the questions that I cared about most deeply, were the same. This could never have happened 10 or 15 years ago. I suspect there are other similarities in other subjects too.

I think the disciplinary boundaries matter less, but this sense of prioritizing certain urgent questions about the possibilities of social order and the role of media information infrastructures in mediating those possibilities, are drawing a lot of people together. That would be an interesting conversation regardless of whatever disciplinary background someone came from.

That leads to the question of the role of the university. It's obvious that the university has been under threat for many reasons related to neoliberalism, general funding cuts, the new model in Britain of trying to move from a publicly subsidized university system to a total market system, and various forms of regulatory mechanisms that get in the way of research. These things have been happening and they are facts.

My view, though, is that it's very important for those of us privileged enough to still have a role within something like a university to not compromise how we exercise that privilege to be uncompromising in talking about the values which motivate our work, motivate our research, and our sense of how we teach, and to communicate those to students without qualification or disguise. That is my commitment and I have yet to find students who don't respond to that. It might be that things will play out differently in different countries, but that's my approach. I think that's the role that academics still have left to them, even if it's just a reserve role that's increasingly diminishing and is under various threats.

**HB**: What is next for Nick Couldry, specifically?

**NC**: We're starting a project about the mediatization of government. That might sound rather grand and pompous, but it's actually about what happens to government on the inside—I mean the work of civil servants, the work of administration, the work of implementing policy on the ground—when the media process—the assumption that what's in the media is going to make a lot more difference than what isn't, and various people have more power over that than others and it may not be you—gets inside the process of government. Do they distort the process of government? Do they undermine politicians' legitimate desire to think about what they need to do in the face of problems, the complexity of which has not been known in previous societies? In other words, I'm interested in the question of whether government, as we would like to understand it, is now possible in an age of profound mediatization. That's one project I'm working on with a colleague.

I'm starting a book with a colleague in Germany which will go back to Berger and Luckmann's sociological classic from the 1960s, *The Social Construction of Reality*, and try to rewrite that bold social-theoretical exploration from the point of view of societies when media are very important. We're going to call it *The Mediated*

*Construction of Reality.* Berger and Luckmann, although they were writing in 1966 and knew that television and radio were there, only mention it very obliquely. It didn't filter into their theory in any way whatsoever, perhaps because it wasn't that important yet. Yes, there were exceptional moments when media mattered, but it just wasn't that important. People could switch off the TV and do all the other stuff. Now there is no switching off because we immediately go on to the next device, which is linking back to what we just saw. We're interested in how to rethink the notion of understanding the construction of social reality from the point of view of societies that are saturated in media, rather than those that, apparently, have no media in them. That's going to be an interesting project.

And I'm becoming chair of the department, so I'll have my hand on the administrative tiller too.

**HB**: Sounds like you won't be getting much sleep.

**NC**: Well, I think it's good to keep busy and I think the challenge of getting clearer about what the main issues are and just trying to speak as directly to those issues as one possibly can, goes on getting more exciting.

**HB**: In your LSE inaugural lecture, which I had the pleasure of viewing on YouTube—this being the wonderfully mediated society that this is—you mentioned several myths. One of them was the myth of big data. I was wondering if you could comment on that.

**NC**: This is a myth that's coming at us quite quickly. It is, in a sense, in a sequence with the older myths about our lives needing to be organized around central media, which I have been talking about. But, in a way, it's of a different sort because it's taking over the whole of the scientific establishment as well. It's not that big data as such is a myth. Clearly there are now capacities to do massive parallel calculations of millions of simultaneous equations generating results, which could not be predicted, but which appear to be able to predict other forms of things we want to understand.

**HB**: Genomics and things like that?

**NC**: Genomics, or market behaviour, or whatever it might be. That's not trivial. Similarly, because so much data is being generated, including by our everyday interactions as they are tracked, the problem of interpreting all that is colossal. It's not just a matter of a boffin sitting down in the headquarters of Google and wondering about what Mr Couldry was saying at 3:20 on a Tuesday afternoon.

That's inconceivable. The scale of the interpretative task is now unimaginably large. That poses a challenge for the sociological imagination. I stress the word "imagination" because there is a risk—this is common idea in a lot of airport books about the wonders of big data—that the academy itself will get taken over by a view that the challenge now for the sciences and the social sciences is just to do more and more calculations, faster and faster, more and more parallel, to generate proxies which will create—although we won't understand what they mean—means of predicting this or that thing that we do want to understand, or we do want to follow, and we'll just plug the data in and rely on that. We'll give up on the act of interpretation.

The editor of Wired, Chris Anderson, an influential figure, wrote an essay in 2007 called *"The End of Theory"*, which was celebrating big theory. He said, *"We don't now need hypotheses. We don't need any form of social science, or even natural science, which tries to interpret whatever the hell is going on out there."*

**HB**: So the idea is that we just need to crunch the numbers?

**NC**: Crunch the numbers. That was his view. It seems like a joke, but that idea is actually being implemented in the skewing of research finance towards that large-scale data crunching and away from qualitative research, away from any form of social science, including big statistical work, which is based around the project of trying to interpret the social as if it was the result of an aggregate of human beings acting. Chris Anderson says in that essay something like, "Who knows why they're doing what they're doing? The point is they're doing it".

**HB**: It doesn't matter.

**NC**: It doesn't matter because we can track it anyway whatever the reason is. Sure, to some extent that's true. For many purposes we don't need to know why people are doing what they're doing. But as a model of understanding society, and therefore as a model of governments looking over the shoulders of social scientists and understanding what they're trying to govern, this is truly catastrophic, because it erases the space of the human subject and the subject that's trying to interpret that other human subject. It discounts what we know about what matters in our lives together. This is a deeply disabling view of social science and it directly contradicts the view of Weber for whom sociology was the science of interpreting human action.

Whatever the boost behind that sort of rhetoric, we have to take it really seriously because if applied in any way at all, it will gradually erase the space of social science, which isn't just a matter of concern for social scientists like myself; rather, it actually provides some of the basic languages for making justice claims and making claims for a new possible politics. Without an adequate social science or the ability to imagine it, we lose the possibility to reimagine the social. Then we really do start to threaten the basis of politics even more fundamentally and totally than a Milton Friedman could have imagined.

**HB**: And it's not only social science. Through this filter you don't have Einstein. You don't have Shakespeare. You don't have Gandhi. You don't have anything.

**NC**: You don't have Darwin. Darwin sat in his garden when he was in his 80s looking at worms and studying the way they moved leaves around, realizing that they had a modicum of intelligence. They did it a certain way and not another. He did that through observation because he wanted to interpret, with an extraordinary vision, the intentions of animals that had not been regarded as having intelligence. Perhaps we could get to some of those conclusions with big data, but not the notion of intention and not the notion of purpose.

This is a big debate across the sciences and I think it has enormous public consequences, but, to make that clearer to the wider public, we have to speak for the university as a place where these types of values are held as important because they relate to underlying human values which are not just those of those lucky enough to pass through our walls.

**HB**: That's a very compelling call to arms. Thank you very much, Nick. It's been a most enjoyable conversation.

**NC**: Thanks a lot, Howard. I've enjoyed it.

## Questions for Discussion:

*1. Do you agree of disagree with Nick's comments regarding the "myth" of big data? Readers interested in this topic are also referred to Chapters 6 and 11 of **The Social World, Reexamined** with Tufts University philosopher Brian Epstein.*

*2. How do you think modern communications technologies will impact the role of the university, both in terms of teaching and its interaction with broader society?*

## Continuing the Conversation

Readers interested in a more detailed understanding of Nick's views are referred to his many books, including: *The Cost of Connection: How Data Is Colonizing Human Life and Appropriating It for Capitalism, Media: Why It Matters, The Mediated Construction of Reality: Society, Culture, Mediatization* (with Andreas Hepp) and *Why Voice Matters: Culture and Politics After Neoliberalism.*

# Ideas Roadshow Collections

Each Ideas Roadshow collection offers 5 separate expert conversations presented in an accessible and engaging format.

- *Conversations About Anthropology & Sociology*
- *Conversations About Astrophysics & Cosmology*
- *Conversations About Biology*
- *Conversations About History, Volume 1*
- *Conversations About History, Volume 2*
- *Conversations About History, Volume 3*
- *Conversations About Language & Culture*
- *Conversations About Law*
- *Conversations About Neuroscience*
- *Conversations About Philosophy, Volume 1*
- *Conversations About Philosophy, Volume 2*
- *Conversations About Physics, Volume 1*
- *Conversations About Physics, Volume 2*
- *Conversations About Politics*
- *Conversations About Psychology, Volume 1*
- *Conversations About Psychology, Volume 2*
- *Conversations About Religion*
- *Conversations About Social Psychology*
- *Conversations About The Environment*
- *Conversations About The History of Ideas*

All collections are available as both eBook and paperback.